Emerging Trends in Indian Marketing in the 90s

edited by :

S. C. SAHOO & P. K. SINHA

Academic Foundation

☆ DELHI ☆

First Published : 1991 by

Academic Foundation

24 - A, Sriram Road, Civil Lines, Delhi - 110 054. (INDIA).

Phone : 232966, 2911852 & 233730.

EMERGING TRENDS IN INDIAN MARKETING

by S. C. Sahoo & P. K. Sinha (Ed.)

ISBN-81-7188-060-6

Laser-Typeset by :

COMPRINT INDIA

24 - A, Sriram Road, Civil Lines, Delhi - 110 054.

Printed at: D.K. FINE ART PRESS, Delhi.

CONTENTS

Continued . . .

EMERGING TRENDS IN INDIAN MARKETING IN THE 90s

CONTENTS

CONTENTS

CONTENTS

CONTENTS

FROM THE PUBLISHER

The New Era of Eighties and Nineties

MARKETING and Promotion — or SELLING — has become the key-word of the present age. Even political parties and their candidates are being sold as products by marketing and advertising agencies through audio, video and all other image-projection aids. The advent of Comparative Advertising has broken all conventions and norms of decency that were earlier followed rigourously in the field of advertising. Day by day, it is becoming a "free for all" atmosphere, the only objective being grabbing the field and pushing others out. But all the same, the intense competitive selling is proving a big boon for the consumer who is really emerging as the king after so many decades of shortages of ordinary, essential consumer products. The range of new products and choices in the market is increasing day by day. Surprisingly enough, the continually rising inflation is proving no hinderance at all to the new market boom — and, above all, we have a real consumer-products boom in the midst of poverty in India. Perhaps all this may magically and wishfully alleviate Indian poverty !

The Consumer scene in India has changed dramatically during the second half of the decade of eighties — a complete transformation of the buyer in India — a virtual metamorphosis — the Indian consumer has really begun to consume, rather with a vengeance. The reasons are many : the massive proliferation of goods and services on the supply side and the pull of prosperity on the demand side — the bubbling prosperity both in the vast rural areas and in the dense urban conglomerates — the unaccounted money from the parallel economy overflowing everywhere. The demonstration effect is inspiring the children, the youth and the women, of all types of households, to go all out and buy by pursuading or coaxing the head of the family to pay for it from savings or current income or through loan. The psychology of inflation is prompting everybody to greedily increase the rates of their services or products to the maximum extent possible from time to time — from short-time to short-time. And thus, we are all caught up in the vicious circle of unbridled consumption and the need to pay for it, by hook or crook — the case of the unemployed and the poor below the poverty line, of course, falls in a different world altogether — beyond the hedge or behind the bush. But all the same, the marketing challenges of the closing decade of the 20th century are to be faced boldly by the professional people. The cyclonic changes preceding the advent of 21st century ought to be forecast to prepare the brave marketer for the big leap...

— Raj Kapila

Director, Academic Foundation

We are glad to present, in this volume, a kaliedoscopic review of emerging trends in Indian marketing in the nineties, covered in fourteen chapters by eleven management and marketing scholars / experts.

FUTURE studies will form a fundamental part of the planning and research activities of marketing managers. Market research is just entering a boom in India and is being embraced with gusto by both the private sector and the government, points out Dr. Atul Parvatiyar in his kingpin article DIMENSIONS OF FUTURE MARKETING IN INDIA (Ch. 1) which virtually refers to all the basic issues involved in the main theme of the book : EMERGING TRENDS IN THE NINETIES.

Services Marketing and Rural Marketing are the areas where there will be more action in the 90s. The marketing idea of consumption without ownership or part ownership will provide new opportunities. Consumer goods made solely with the needs and resources of rural consumers in mind, will have to be designed. During the NINETIES marketing will also be more socially responsible, legally constrained, value-oriented, flexible, anticipatory and conservation-oriented. The future development is expected in non-traditional areas such as the marketing of health care, arts, financial schemes, insurance, universities and their courses and professions. With the cost of living outstripping increases in income, consumers will become more value-conscious. Durable goods will have to be designed with a view to reducing the average annual cost of ownership. Deceptive selling, shabby products, false sales promises, poor services in case of durable products and high price fixing — these practices will have to be abandoned in the nineties, asserts Dr. Parvatiyar.

THE competitive decade of eighties has left very little doubt about the importance of marketing in an emerging buyers' market. With increasing education and media exposure, consumer demand for quality, safety and hygiene will continue to escalate, cautions Mr. Khokan Mookerji in his cogent, comprehensive and revealing article TOWARDS NEW HORIZONS IN MARKETING (Ch.3).

While the wife / mother has already been established as an important source of authority, both teenagers and children are becoming new sources of influence with its attendant demands on manufacturers to fashion products and communication to these target groups.

Time pressures will impinge on the recommendatory role of the urban retailer, hence the need to create brands which rely less on trade PUSH and more on consumer PULL, specially when there will be diminishing dealer / retailer loyalty with increased competition amongst products.

Two thirds of the population of India has been exposed to TV. This has kindled new wants and desires. However, the majority will not have the means of fulfilling the newly aroused needs. Hence, the marketers have to be very cautious about the frightening possibilities of people with champagne thirsts and Campa Cola purses, warns Mr. Mookerji.

1980s has been the decade of very fast growth in the number of products being introduced. The liberalization of government policy with regard to technology - transfer gave an impetus to the world's best technology flowing into the country. Consequently the housewife is on to an electronic trip and will go for everything that reduces her workload. But 1990s, the pre-runner to the 21st Century, will be a different decade than the last. We shall be entering, not into a market place, but into an arena in 1990s, says Dr. P.K. Sinha in his paper on INDIAN MARKET IN THE NINETIES (Ch.2.).

KENNEDY'S Presidential Message of 1962 declared that consumers had the right to safety, to be informed, to choose, and to be heard. That paved the way for consumer protection legislation and movement in U.S.A. and other developed countries. The consumer movement in India is in its infancy and is largely confined to metropolitan cities. But consumerism has certainly acquired momentum and shall pose a challenge to our industry and trade in the days to come. What should be the tasks and programmes for the companies to respond to the growing consumerism ? Prof. S.C. Sahoo poses this question and then answers it in his paper CONSUMERISM : CHALLENGES AND TASKS FOR 90s (Ch.4).

THE rural market, which is vast but relatively untapped, has thrown a big challenge to the marketers, and when met, will bring a new era of prosperity to the country. Such healthy, high hopes are raised by S.K. Patro in his paper on RURAL MARKET CHALLENGES (Ch.5.).

THE consumer durables' and non-durables' rural market has generated increased potential not because of the initiatives of Indian marketers but due to the 'pull' from the consuming system caused by spurt in agrarian prosperity. While pointing this out in his empirical research paper on EMERGING CONSUMER MARKETS (Ch.6), Prof. V. Mukunda Das emphasises that the study of the evolution of rural consuming system becomes highly relevant in developing countries like India and reveals how the consuming systems adjust to such spurts in material prosperity.

THE new set up of European Market will be the most

important single economic event in the early nineties. The twelve countries of Europe will emerge as an economic union and may build a fortress which the developing countries like India may find difficult to penetrate. It is here that a suitable export strategy requires to be worked out, says Prof. S.C. Sahoo in his article on EXPORT MARKETS (Ch.7).

The manufacturing sector is shrinking in the Western industrialised countries in terms of its contribution to GNP. The U.S. and other industrialised countries will, therefore, need manufactured products which could be supplied by "new-comers" including India. What Korea, Taiwan and Mexico could do, India could also do, (and should try to do better) opines Prof. Sahoo, if the policy undergoes a change.

THE majority of the successful small-scale units are satellites of large business houses. This is the significant remark made by Mohan Agrawal in his article on EXPORT MARKETS FOR SMALL-SCALE INDUSTRIES (Ch.8).

THERE is a virtual absence of "Research Culture" among most of the Indian companies. But during the Nineties the research will have to be made an integral part of marketing, proclaims Dr. P.K. Sinha in his paper on MARKETING RESEARCH (Ch.9).

ABOUT 180 million of the rural population have purchasing power but only a small portion of them can be reached through mass media — less than half of them are literate. Only 100 million adults in the rural areas are, thus, the target consumers. Almost all advertising and marketing efforts in India are aimed at this section of the population. The product competition will be so intense that it would create increasing industrial sickness of medium and small units. Stagnation of markets is, therefore, predicted by J.S. Giri Rao and D. Panigrahy in their paper on MASS COMMUNICATION AND INDIAN CONSUMER (Ch. 10).

THE decade of Eighties saw the beginning of the "Positioning Era", Comparative Advertising, Political Advertising, the growing importance of Shelf Space at retail outlets, the importance of rural markets and the beginnings of the conception of "Direct Marketing" as a philosophy. All these were governed by a common denominator — a quantum increase in competition. The Nineties should see the crystallisation of these changes, says Prof. S. Govindrajan in his paper on PROMOTION (Ch.11).

IN the consumer products, impulse buying is gaining momentum — about 40 per cent of the consumers buying on impulse. The only way this phenomenon can be exploited is through "Point of Purchase" displays. Therefore, all large and keen competitors are trying to win space in the shops, points out Dr. P.K. Sinha in his paper on POP DISPLAY (Ch.12).

THE future of banking lies in identifying customer needs and developing new ways of satisfying them. Bankers have to study the motives, habits, feelings and preferences of their customers if they are to become truely marketing oriented, explains Ranjan Kumar Bal in his paper on BANK MARKETING (Ch.13).

MARKETING'S critical role in development will be appreciated only when it meets the needs of the present without compromising the ability of future generations to meet their own needs. Society cannot afford to waste and deplete resources. The foremost involvement of marketing in the conserver approach, therefore, is to diversify demand away from products and services which are materials-wasteful and energy intensive. In his paper on CONSERVER MARKETING (Ch.14), Prof. Atul Parvatiyar, therefore, emphasises that marketing's role in a world of resource shortages is to promote their more efficient use.

— R. K.

Foreword

THE National Seminar on Marketing in the Nineties, organised by Bhubaneswar Management Forum, was an interesting effort in a study of Emerging Trends in Indian Marketing. It gave an opportunity to management academicians, administrators and managers from industry to discuss in width and depth this subject of great importance to the country. Marketing is the core of the economy, surrounded by finance, production, logistics and other functions. On a sound marketing system depends our growth. A healthy marketing system is always responsive to the consumer and the society for goods and services, efficiency and low cost.

I am therefore glad that this publication has been brought out by Academic Foundation as a contribution to management thought and interest in the country.

— PRAKASH TANDON

PRESIDENT,
NATIONAL COUNCIL OF APPLIED ECONOMIC RESEARCH

Introduction

— RANGAN CHAKRAVARTY*

THE decade of the eighties has witnessed a revolution in the Indian market. The growth of an affluent urban population, estimated to be no less than 180 million, has led to complex patterns of development that provide material for a fascinating study.

We've seen new products meeting with major successes, small-time operators shaking up established multi-nationals, television emerging as 'the' medium with newer and newer relay stations and satellite links spreading its network across the country.

We've also seen new 'cultures' being talked about — whether it is Maruti or Pan Parag ! The emergence of Indian brands has tallied with a spirit of 'Mera Bharat Mahan' and the result has been dozens of 'nationalist' commercials on the 'all-Indian' theme.

The growth of semi-urban markets, emergence of small towns and rural buying power, have all posed fresh challenges to the producer-marketer. The transition from a seller's market to a buyer's market in certain key categories has demanded a new, lean and hungry management style for survival in a competitive jungle (as the IAS has slowly been replaced by the Management Graduate in the marriage market).

But behind all this euphoria there has been a deep sense of premonition. Because under all the waves of glitter

---

* Sr. Creative Director, Clarion Advertising Services Ltd., Calcutta.

and gloss there has been a deep dark ocean of under-development, of poverty and illiteracy.

This has given marketing operations a frenzied sense of urgency born out of a realization of the transience. The saturation in consumer durable markets, the death of many a brands of television etc., have deepened such worries.

On the other hand, increased money power and money-awareness have led to a series of investment opportunities and the success of mega issues. Diversifications have become the order of the day, laying new emphasis on the importance of adaptability for 'inter-field' operations in large corporate bodies.

Emerging Trends in Indian Marketing in the Nineties is a pioneering effort in scanning these aspects and probing the implications towards developing a complete understanding of the situation.

Here is an exciting study of an enticing subject, edited with rare care.

Preface

INDIAN marketing is characterised by diversities, making a marketing manager work for his money ; though diversified, it was static. Then came the technological collaborations, and the life style of the people changed. It was true to the phrase : *Turning a new Leaf.* Unforeseen changes occured and the era of marketing dawned in India. The market accepted all the products with both hands. There was a mushroom growth in the industrial sector. Consumers started getting the choice they never before had. In the process they became quality conscious and very pronounced in their acceptance or rejection. Consumerism arrived and market started consolidating. Competition became intense causing several to go out of reckoning. The technology was no more the key to success. Then came 1990 and everybody started guesstimating the changes that might occur in the decade and after. This book is an attempt in this direction.

The book contains fourteen articles covering several aspects of marketing. The first six deal with the foreseen changes that are likely to occur in the Indian urban as well as rural marketing environment. The next two relate to the perceived changes as well as the strategies needed for success in the export market. Market Research being the heart of any marketing effort has also been included in the volume. The recent trends have put promotion in the fore-front to achieve a good customer rapport. Hence, three articles have been included to deal with mass communication, changing scene of promotion and POP display strategies. Services are going to play a major role in the Indian economy. Being one of the oldest and the largest service industries, Bank Marketing has been chosen for this volume. Keeping pace with the ecological needs an attempt has been made in the last article to find out and suggest the role marketing can play in the conservation of environment for a sustainable development of the economy.

The authors have tried to express their views on the likely changes, in the time to come, in the marketing scenario and to examine the implications thereof. They have also endeavoured to suggest strategies to meet successfully the challenges posed. However, the ultimate test of the usefulness of this book lies in the level of its acceptance by the comity of students, managers, teachers and trainers. We would feel amply rewarded if the book meets their expectations.

— S. C. Sahoo
P. K. Sinha

Acknowledgements

THIS edited volume is the result of our participation in a national seminar on **Marketing : 90s** organised by the Bhubaneswar Management Forum and the encouragement received from the deliberations of the participants, most prominent being Prakash Tondon, President, Board of Governors, National Council of Applied Economic Research; Hardeep Singh, Polar International; Khokan Mookerji, ITC Limited; P.H. Rao, Crompton Greaves Limited and Ashok Singh, the Convenor of the Forum. We express our deep sense of gratitude to them and the organisers of the seminar.

We owe our deep indebtedness also to our esteemed contributors who have timely responded to our request and joined with us in this venture. If it is a success, the credit goes to each one of them.

Our special thanks are to Rangan Chakravarty, Senior Creative Director, Clarion Advertising, for writing a befitting Introduction to the book.

We are equally grateful to Prof. Soubhagya K. Misra and Prof. N. Mohanty of the Post-Graduate Department of English, Berhampur University, who spared their most valued time in editing the articles included in the present volume.

We shall fail in our duty if we do not acknowledge our indebtedness to Mrs. Bijaya Sahoo and Mrs. Jyotsna Sinha for having patiently and smilingly borne the brunt of domestic responsibilities and provided all encouragement. Mrs. Sinha deserves special thanks for going through the first draft of the manuscript.

Our thanks are due to Lingaraj Pattanaik (Lulu) for all secretarial assistance unhesitatingly offered.

We are grateful to our publishers, Academic Foundation, for bringing out the book in a nice get-up and that too within the shortest possible time.

— *S.C.S & P.K.S*

The Contributors

ATUL PARVATIYAR
Xavier Labour Relations Institute (XLRI), Jamshedpur.

KHOKAN MOOKERJI
General Manager, (Marketing Services), ITC Limited, Calcutta.

S. C. SAHOO
Department of Business Administration, Berhampur University.

V. MUKUNDA DAS
Institute of Rural Management, Anand, Gujarat.

P. K. SINHA
Xavier Institute of Management, Bhubaneswar.

MOHAN L. AGRAWAL
Xavier Labour Relations Institute (XLRI), Jamshedpur.

S. GOVINDRAJAN
Xavier Institute of Management, Bhubaneswar.

S. K. PATRO
Department of Business Administration, Berhampur University.

J. S. GIRI RAO
Department of Journalism & Mass Comm., Berhampur University.

RANJAN KUMAR BAL
Department of Business Administration, Utkal University.

D. PANIGRAHI
Department of Business Administration, Berhampur University.

1

Dimensions of Future Marketing in India

ATUL PARVATIYAR

Dr. Parvatiyar has made an attempt to highlight the recent developments in Indian marketing. He has identified the directions that are likely to have a positive impact on marketing planning and practices. Marketing will be more socially responsible, legally constrained and value-oriented in the decades to come. Marketing of non-traditional items like health care, arts, financial schemes, insurance, universities and their courses, professions, etc. will witness a tangible development. The author has convincingly put *Personnel* and *Probe* as two additional elements of the marketing-mix which so far consisted of 4Ps. He expects a qualitative change in marketing research, since, according to him, *Probe* is a vital element to be taken help of while designing any marketing strategy. The influence and role of women had to be given due recognition by the marketers. Towards the end of his paper, Prof. Parvatiyar foresees servicing to witness the greatest rise among all the dimensions of marketing strategy. He sincerely expects consumers' consciousness to improve, and pre-sale and post-sale services and warranty assurances to be demanded by consumers.

— *EDITORS*

MARKETING development in India is likely to move in several directions in the years to come. The changing environment will influence not only the nature of strategic marketing practices but also the field of marketing itself. The purpose of this paper is to highlight recent developments and identify fundamental directions which will have

Printed with permission from the Editor, *Management and Labour Studies*, a quarterly journal of Xavier Labour Relations Institute, Jamshedpur where this paper was first published.

an enduring effect upon the practice of marketing in India, in the decades immediately ahead.

Indications are that, in the future, marketing will be more socially responsible, legally constrained, value-oriented, flexible, anticipatory and conservation-oriented.[1] Most prognostications suggest intensive future development in non-traditional areas such as the marketing of health care, arts, financial schemes, insurance, universities and their courses and professions.[2]

Looking at current trends in the general practice of marketing, one is apt to say that new ways of marketing will continue to evolve. With the array of changes in information technology and growing interest in international markets, we will follow close on the heels of the developed countries in the use of sophisticated marketing techniques and tools. Research will gain importance among Indian marketers and researching methods themselves will undergo a change.

Socially Responsible Marketing

Marketing strategy appears to be becoming more ethical because of the public demand for socially responsible business and the perception that ethical marketing practices bear fruit in the long run. Deceptive selling, shabby products, false sales promises, poor services in case of many durable products and high price fixing have been among the practices of fringe operators and are sometimes included even in the procedures of reputed companies. These questionable practices have provoked a sustained consumer movement and also *customer-protection* legislation from the government.

To cope with ethical challenges, attempts by marketers may take several forms. Marketing management may sponsor Consumer Conferences in order to deal with consumer complaints. This is intended to act as a parallel consumer movement sponsored by the marketing organization itself. Already a few companies in India, such as Bajaj Electricals, State Bank of India and others, have started this practice.

Marketing management will also resort to more research and measurement in the pursuit of *actuality*. Marketing scholars as well as practitioners are likely to give consideration to professional behaviour. Enhanced professionalism requires marketing behaviour guided by a code of ehtics.[3]

The development of a useful code of ethics or some other method of professional control should, therefore, be a major concern of marketers in the next decade. In the light of increased government willingness to prosecute illegalities and the propensity of the press to publicize unethical business practices, the use of an *ethics committee* or of *ethical consultants* will guide marketing decisions. Companies may also conduct periodic seminars on ethics for their marketing executives enabling them to discuss the social and ethical dimensions of strategic marketing decisions.

Constrained Marketing

Marketing strategy in the next decade will probably be more constrained. Increased government regulations, prosecutions, negative publicity and the growing strength of consumerism are indications of a future marketing strategy, which will be more cautious, vigilant, and, therefore, constrained. Restrictions will be imposed on the kind of copy and the media that can be used to promote certain products, especially in the case of advertising aimed at children and featuring women as models.

To ensure greater safety and product integrity, product research and testing will increase. The cost of increased product testing, expanded warranty programmes, regulated changes in packaging and labelling, observance of environmental standards and other mandatory requirements may pass on to the consumer. The upward pressure on prices due to the cost of complying with such regulations might somewhat limit the growth of sales. On the other hand, some restrictive legislations will be reduced. For instance, regulations on foreign investments and technical collaborations, tax reliefs and incentives by the government to certain type of industries like electronics have already been substantially relaxed. As a result, competition has increased and prices have been reduced, expanding the total market.

Value-oriented Marketing

Resource shortages, taxes, inflation and costly efforts to maintain the quality of the physical environment will raise the cost of goods and services. With the cost of living (particularly housing and energy) outstripping increases in income,[4] consumers will become more value conscious in the future. They will analyze the benefits of their purchases, become more price conscious and, therefore, more discriminatory.

The implications for marketers would be to go in for more value-oriented products. Durable goods will have to be designed to last longer and serviced easily with a view to reducing the average annual cost of ownership. Though there will be frequent style changes in the immediate future, primarily because of the Japanese entry into the Indian markets and their strategy of continuous product development, modular components will be designed for easy serviceability.

Consumers may forego certain services to obtain merchandise at the lowest price.[5] Price efficient substitute products will be sought after. Direct selling will increase, when economically efficient. Because of the profound impact of continuing inflation on marketing, tangible benefit-oriented marketing strategies will grow. Emotional appeals to buyers are likely to be reduced. A specific example is the industry's effort to produce more energy-efficient appliances and the emphasis on energy efficiency in promotion.

Conserver Marketing

In a world of growing ecological concern and the emerging crisis of resource shortages, marketing will become more conservation oriented in the coming years. Promoting the conservation ethos is both socially desirable and a perceived ecological necessity.[6]

Flexible Marketing

Marketing strategy in coming years will have to be more flexible and adaptable. The major factor in enhancing flexibility is the rapid development of the new technology. Business firms able to make rapid use of technological breakthroughs in their operations will have profitable opportunities. Slow paced enterprises will confront disadvantages and may be locked out of certain markets.

Decentralization of production in smaller units will be advantageous by reducing transportation costs and the inherent inefficiencies associated with large organisation.

Recent developments like the following would have a considerable effect on marketing in India.

Microprocessors

Because of these chips, a wave of smart products are being introduced in the consumer market. Among these are pocket calculators, television computer games, digital watches, telephones with programmed numbers and programmed credit cards. There is also a growing demand for such products in this market. However, at the same time, the market is very volatile with production costs and prices constantly being reduced and new and improved products continuously being introduced.

Information Technology

With the development of information technology and the growing use of computers, an increasing number of marketing decisions will be based on the information thus provided. Not only would information storage and retrieval for marketing purposes increase, but new strategic marketing opportunities may also be seized. Thus the Diner's Club has found a marketing opportunity by providing syndicated market research data based on its members' profile records. Citibank has provided computer terminals at clients' premises for easy transactions with the bank and also to provide consolidated statements to the clients. Bata is using a computer network between its retail stores, the factory and the Head Office to improve physical distribution and logistics planning.

One of the recent developments in marketing methods in the West is telephone selling and tele-training on product updates. Indian marketers, primarily those interested in international markets, will find in these a new channel of distribution and selling.

The establishment of major cable television systems with multichannel offerings and specialized programming permits alert firms to reach certain segmented audiences more easily than through national network television.

Anticipatory Marketing

Change is the certainty of future. Rapid social, economic and technological changes will make marketing strategy anticipatory. There will be greater efforts to forecast short and such like. Perhaps more rigorous efforts will be made to forecast the long-term demand for industrial goods and components. The debacle of many large chemical plants like caustic soda plants which were expanded due to booming demand in the mid 1970s[7] and faced stagnating markets thereafter, will make industries more cautious in future.

Individuals with background in future studies will be particularly valuable to the planning and research activities of marketing managers. Market research is just entering a boom in India.[8] It is being embraced with gusto by both the private sector and the government. The activity will continue to grow and research operations are likely to change radically.

The use of multivariate techniques and computer software for market research will increase and the very nature of marketing research will change and newer techniques will develop. The methodological changes in marketing research design will provide marketing research professionals with the opportunity to design decision support system (DSS) for their firms. A decision support system is a system that turns data into information to improve decision-making. It permits decisions to be efficiently tracked and the ideal DSS can be directly used by decision-makers such as the product manager.[9]

There will also be improvements in the process of data collection for market research. Various computer assisted mechanisms for data collection will be used. Experimental variable manipulation and other optimization techniques which are being used in Japan may soon become popular in India too. In this method, between 30 and 40 variables are being manipulated at one time, adding new dimensions to factor analysis.[10]

Marketing academics will have to explore new dimensions in their research. In research on purchasing decisions, they will have to address themselves to the intensive study of the important ecological factors. Increasingly researchers will have to look for new ideas not through consumer research alone, but also through scenario analysis and creative action.[11]

Broadened Marketing

One of the more pronounced developments of the present decade, and one that promises to continue strongly in the future, is the broadened application of marketing techniques in public and non-profit sectors. Hospitals, arts organizations, educational institutions, banks, public sector organizations, and social service groups are applying marketing much in the same manner as private corporations. Marketing methods have been used to help disseminate family planning, to attract investment in public sector companies, to popularize political candidates and parties, and to increase the acceptability of a social idea. Indicative of some of the applications of marketing in the service sector are the following examples :

Health Care Marketing

In the last few years, a number of commercial hospitals and diagnostic units have come up in India. Even corporate hospitals like Appolo and Batra's are becoming popular. Extensive marketing campaigns have begun to educate Indians on the value of preventive care. In coming years, hospitals will use marketing in an attempt to increase occupancy and reduce cost. Strategies for international marketing of health care to Arab countries will attract attention because of its great potential. A host of health care related industries like pharmaceutical and drugs, medical electronic equipments, etc, will also benefit.

Packaged Environment Marketing

With the growth of tourism and the application of marketing techniques to attract more foreign and domestic tourists, new marketing ideas are also in the offing. Packaged Environments, like *Appu Ghar* are an indication of marketing advances. The Packaged Environment concept will be applied to market theme parks, enclosed shopping malls, sports and cultural centres and select hotels, restaurants and retail stores. The concept starts with the marketing objective that the theme setting translates into quality, convenience, comfort or enjoyment, by the use of art, architecture, audio aids and atmosphere.

Forseeing the Next Ten Years

Services Marketing and rural marketing are the areas where the action will be over the next decade. The future holds rewards for service businesses.[12] The marketing idea of consumption without ownership or part ownership will provide new opportunities.[13] In future, marketers will have to visualize marketing of *experiences* as their key products instead of the traditional goods and services. The customer will not be sold tourist products. Instead, he will be provided with an experience of living in a particular *period*, or in a custom created fanciful *dream situation*.

The marketing of services will also face new challenges. A major challenge will be to find a balance between offering a service and selling a product. Preserving the integrity of the service when it has been transformed into a product will require special attention. Human resource management and marketing management will have to be closely interlinked in the services business. A service organization will need product, people, client, management people, and sales people. In future, service will have to look at new channels of distribution; they will have to advertise, embark on public relations programmes and promotion programmes besides the formal sales campaigns.[14]

Rural marketing deserves a fresh look. With a lot of development activities in progress in the rural areas and the national television network expanding to reach more and more of the rural population marketers will find these markets more economical to reach and service than before. But the type of rural marketing hitherto practiced by most organizations will require change. The present focus has been on rural distribution through existing channels and development of agro-based products. Consumer goods made solely with the needs and resources of rural customers in mind, have not yet been designed. In future, attention will be on developing new products and new channels of distribution in the rural areas. More research on the impact of various forms of advertising in rural areas will be commissioned.

Marketers have also begun to acknowledge women's new role. They have got the message that women are important target groups who influence consumer purchases. There is a growing realization that all women are not home makers, and that even the home makers are not centred solely on their homes. The recognition of working women, including executives, has been slow in coming, lagging well behind the demographic shift of women into the workforce.

Marketers can keep up with women if they regard the market as a moving target that continues to change. Today women have more options and choices, and there is a greater diversity of values and life styles among them.[15]

Changing Marketing Strategy

Marketing-mix components, which have a direct bearing on the choice of marketing strategy, will also undergo changes along with changes in the market and in society. The composition of the marketing-mix will be based not only on the traditional 4Ps - Product, Price, Place and Promotion. *Personnel* and *Probe* will be added to the 4Ps as essential elements of the marketing-mix.

Considering *Probe* as the fifth P of the marketing-mix will encourage organizations to adopt research into the impact that information gathering and analysis have on demand. Soliciting consumer suggestions, conducting future studies, and establishing a formal cooperative marketing research programme, constitute a controllable, tactical decision, which has a direct impact on demand.[16]

The importance of personnel, those associated with the product, with client management, or sales, has greatly increased. It deserves the status of marketing's sixth P. Personnel form the key to the creation, delivery and servicing of market offerings to consumers. A firm's image and positioning is very much influenced by its personnel. Also, sales representatives will, in future, play the exciting role of *customer relations manager*. There will be an increasing demand for highly qualified consultants, because top-level sales negotiations with purchasers will require an increasing degree of competence. In addition, customer management, such as complaint handling, will be more important.

The relative importance of product development, pricing, promotion, distribution and servicing will undergo changes. Technical product research and test marketing will have an edge over product development efforts aimed at style and fashion. Nevertheless, less importance given to style does not mean that the appearance of products will have no value.

Pricing will be under constraints due to rules and regulations of the government. Dubious promotional efforts will be curbed. Image building and advocacy advertising will increase. The effectiveness of promotion will get more attention. Automation in distribution activities will bring about cost efficiency. Transportation, warehousing, inventory control and coordination of middlemen will become important components of the distribution system. Servicing will experience the greatest rise among all the dimensions of marketing strategy. Value consciousness and ethical and conserver marketing will contribute to the rising importance of serving. Pre- and post-sale services and warranty assurances will be demanded by consumers.

REFERENCES

1. Ahmad, Abrar: "Emerging Dimensions of Marketing Management in India", *Proceedings of Second Inter-Institutional Meet of Marketing Managers and Instructors*, Varanasi, April, 1986.

2. Laczinak, GR and Murphy, PE: "Marketing and Performing Arts", *Atlanta Economic Review*, 27, November, 1977, pp. 4-9.

3. Such a code of ethics was discussed in the First Conference of the Indian Marketing Association held at Varanasi in April 1986. A committee of the Association is studying the code of ethics of the American Marketing Association.

4. *Business India*, December 29, 1986, January 11, 1987, p. 41.

5. An example is the success of "Nirma".

6. For details on Conserver Marketing see the author's article "Ecological Perspectives of Marketing in the 1990s: Conserver Marketing for Sustainable Development" published in the present book.

7. *Business India*, December 1-14, 1986, p. 58.

8. *India Today*, November 15, 1986, p. 130.

9. Knuckles, Barbara M, "New Techniques and Changes in Research Design - Their Impact on the Brand and Advertising Development Decision Process", *Journal of Advertising Research*, October-November, 1986, pp. 6-7.

10. Ibid.

11. Houston, Franklin S: "The Marketing Concept: What It Is and What It Is Not".

12. Ceberzynski, Greg: "Challenges Await Service Business", *Marketing News*, AMA, Chicago, November 8, 1985, p. 20.

13. Arora, AP : "Consumption without Ownership: Marketing Opportunities for Tomorrow", *Proceedings of Second Inter- Institutional Meet of Marketing Managers and Instructors*, Varanasi, April, 1986.

14. Ceberzynski, Greg: Op. cit.

15. Langer, Judith : "At Last, Marketers Acknowledge Women's Role", *Marketing News*, AMA, Chicago, November 8, 1985, p. 45.

16. Traynor, Kenneth: "Research Deserves Status as Marketing's Fifth `P'", *Marketing News*, AMA, Chicago, November 8, 1985, p. 7.

Courtesy :

Management and Labour Studies, Vol. 13, No. 1, January, 1988.

2

Indian Market — 1990s

P.K. SINHA

An humble attempt has been made in the present paper to highlight the changes that are likely to take place in the Indian marketing scenario in the 1990s. The author very rightly maintains that over 3/4th of the population will be in their spending years and the emergence of nuclear family will change the spending habits. The customer-population shall be better educated, better informed and quality conscious. They will have greater purchasing power. The 90s will witness the proliferation of products. Companies will like to give a better life to their customers. Services will emerge as a major sector. The author expects that product positioning will be replaced by brand positioning. Since the Indian market for the rich is likely to enlarge, the products meant for prestige and status will be on the increase. A whole lot of addition to the services at the retail outlets such as Credit Cards, Home Deliveries, etc. are foreseeble. As regards promotion, the author argues that for LIPS, POP Displays will play a crucial role and for HIPS, personalised marketing will be emphasised. Shop displays, contests, cooperative ads., etc. will form an important part of dealer promotion. In the rural areas, hoardings and wall paintings will continue to be the leading media. In the urban areas, exhibitions and fairs will be the common scene for promoting the products. Marketing will be more consumer-based with an added social concern. The implementation of the consumer protection laws will be more strict. At the end, Dr. Sinha has given some practical guidelines which may be borne in mind by the Indian marketeers while designing a strategy for the 1990s.

— EDITORS

THE Indian market has been experiencing changes that have left the marketers gaping and only those who could match the speed have succeeded. This trend is expected to contine in 1990s also. This paper is an attempt to highlight the expected changes in Indian marketing in 1990s.

Demographics

India has predominantly been a country of people with an alarmingly huge population of over 800 million. By the end of 90s it will be touching the magical figure of 1000 million. This means so many mouths to feed and so many minds to think. It is the world's second largest customer base and adding to the population. Majority are born after independence. In a sense they are free Indian citizens. This means that majority (over 3/4th) of them will be in the age bracket of 25-50, the spending years. This bracket has and will tend to have the maximum discretionary income and hence the target of all producers. The conversion, therefore, towards a nuclear family breaking up the joint family, is changing the spending habits and is adding to the spendings. The tendency to have a multi-income household is another factor adding to the larger customer base. The population is looking upward and is better educated, better informed and quality conscious. The mobility towards urban area is still unchecked and growing. The *Nagars* are becoming *Mahanagars* (like Colas becoming Mahacolas). This has resulted in a class of people, called a middle class, that is the largest in the world: Over 300 million and growing rapidly. This is the class marketers are vying for. It has a massive purchasing power, rather an enhanced one, through different easy purchase schemes and supports from the financial institutions.

Traditionally, India is a rural based country. Sixty five per cent of the population live there. But they account for only 35 per cent of the total spendings (purchases). These are the people who are still thought to be orthodox. It is not that they have no discretionary income but till recently they didn't have avenues to spend. The change in media scene has changed their spendings and producers are looking forward to them as the latest find in markets that is an ocean. Their *Ideal Consumption Basket* is changing. They are no more as inclined to buy land and gold as they were. Their preference bases have shifted to durables like TVs, vehicles, etc. This tendency has led to the division of the rural area into three developmental stages:[1]

(1) Primary, the true village.
(2) Developing, the upward looking village.
(3) Urban analogous, the deceptive village.

With better facilities through Green and White Revolutions and now with the new government policy to channelize 50 per cent investment into rural areas the number of developing and urban analogous villages will rise rapidly and there is going to be an insurge of their purchasing power.

Psychographics

Traditional ways of looking at target audience in terms of demographics are becoming inadequate with a need to rely more on a whole set of lifestyle classifications[2]. The change to nuclear family has led to democratic purchase decisions with housewife exerting greater influence. The importance of working women is leading to a more prosperous and hedonist life style. The increasing literacy rate and exposure to the world around has given the population a multi-culture orientation. With urbanization, a segment that is comfortable with products based on Western or Indian ethos has emerged. The household is now made of electronic gadgets that were once *dreams* in Indian homes.

The middle class is a typical phenomenon. The rich get everything as and when they want. The poor know that these can not be fulfilled and hence do not dream. Its is only the middle class that dreams and tries to catch a mirage. Its life style has been changed by the convenient payment alternatives and increased discretionary income that help realise its dreams. The bureaucratic look has changed to a dynamic professionalization. The fact that even the entrepreneurs are young and dynamic has changed the industry scene and the market is proliferated with product which have takers. The children want ice-creams and chocolates and that too only Kwality and Cadbury's. Such discretion was never seen before. The child is, literally, going to be the Father of Man. It is tending to be the influencer, if not the decider. Even the villages are affected by the process of change. Hero Honda and ONIDA have become household names. As indicated earlier the villagers' *Ideal Consumption Basket* is changing.

The population is no more homogenous. Every individual is being treated as a segment. The trend seems to be heading to a stage of *Maxi-marketing* where companies will try to gather maximum information about the customers so as to make the offer most suitable to each one of them, individually. The benefit segmentation will give way to occasion segmentation, as seen in ready made garments being offered as casual or formal wear.

Products

1980s has been the decade of a very fast growth in the number of products being introduced, both in terms of range and variety. The liberalization of the government's policy with regard to technology transfer gave an impetus to the world's best technology flowing into the country. One of the main reasons for the change in the life style of the Indian populace is the proliferation of products generated by the technology inflow. Indian products are in no way less than those available outside. In fact, the outflow of such products is increasing day by day.

The main upsurge, though all around, has been in consumer products : durables and consumables. The market that was characterised by a handful of brands and one main brand is a scene of the past. The housewife is no longer satisfied with manual work. She is on to an electronic trip and will go for everything that reduces her workload. The products that increase her leisure time will always be preferred. Electronic gadgets are a part of life. Personal transport is a necessity. Dependence on public transport will increase due to the distance between workplace and home, but a private transport will be a necessity. Cycle will still be the maximum selling vehicle. The number of two-wheelers and car owners will also increase.

On the organisational front, the office automation drive will be faster and surer. The apathy toward it will disappear and even the homes will have computers for their children. Better technologies will ask for and lead to better utilization of the available resources and an intensive search for cheaper/better alternatives. With the privatization of some public sector units, the professionalism is on the rise and more and more companies will perform better to assure the customer of a better life.

A major shift in the product policies that would be evident is the emergence of services as a separate, and perhaps a major sector. The technology boom has given the customers better quality products, but, in the process, the products have become complex in nature requiring expert knowledge to maintain and repair. This is also clear from the fact that for payment of a sum, the person is saved of the trouble of going through the exercises of utilizing the public services. Due to the specialized needs of the organization a tendency to hire a specialist organisation is on the rise. Even the households will depend on specialized services and will find it easier to assign the job to some agency. Better communication techniques will add to it.

With the fight for more personalised product, brand loyalty will be debated. A *cent-off* coupon will be a common trap. The strategy will move from *Product Positioning* to *Brand Positioning*. The brand image will gain primacy. This will also form the basis of diversification. Family brand may not be popular but each brand will have a shelter of a Corporate Image.

The trend shall also be of shift from product to commodity - a situation where there is hardly any product differentiation. The only dividing line between them will be the brands. The frills/feature will be overlooked. The main cause will be overcapacity, sometimes created by a fall in demand but frequently due to the Rubber Type Market[3]. The product with a price that could be massaged and managed and profits which rose with the learning curve, reducing the costs as cumulative production increased, will become at the worst, a license to lose money, at the best a cow, to be worked as long as there is anything in the udder[4]. In order to be successful, the quality will have to be combined with volume. The biggest will be treated as the best.

Due to the fast spread of technology the distinctiveness of the product will be shortlived. However, the products which are meant for prestige only will be on the rise as the market for the riches is growing[5].

Role of Price

The market is tending to move from growth to maturity stage. Majority of the products will be either in their late growth or early growing maturity stage. In such a situation, prices will be modified and used as a major tool to shift. Comparatively the new products will be offered at much less price than today. Though the inflationary pressure and the cost of basic materials will add to the cost, the relative price will be lower. That is, the margin will be lower and the only way to better margin will be cost reduction, without compromising with quality. The companies which look to price as a cost related determination will have to change to the *non-related factors*. As John Winkler states, "Too many companies try and run their businesses on the basis of keeping their prices stable. This is particularly true with the small companies. It might also be one of the reasons why they stay small"[6]. He indicates to the fact that price should be as flexible as the need of the customers and hence cost may be a secondary basis of setting the price.

Indian market is experiencing a peculiar phenomenon now-a-days. The consumer durables have good image when priced higher, as in the case of TVs. On the other hand, PCs marketers are cutting prices like anything and if the response to the price cut by Electronic Corporation is any indication of the things to come, PCs are going to be still cheaper. These are clear indications that price is no longer a cost-related decision. It will be more of the discretion of the Marketing Department than the Finance Department. The consumers will also be price conscious, except for two segments of people, the riches and the new entrants to such market e.g. the villages that are developing towards becoming urban analogous.

Distribution

Although some product classes are well into their maturity the Indian Market is and will be in growth stage. This calls for making available the product in every corner of the market. This is more true with Low Involvement Products (LIPS), where there is a lot of impulse buying (as of now it is 38 per cent, varying among product classes and it is expected to rise). Customers are more likely to go for conveniently available brands. In such a situation, distribution plays a vital role.

The retail marketing will not be the same dull exercise. The shops will have to have good get ups. The salesperson will have to be a professional. The personal service shops will make way for the departmental stores where consumers will find it convenient and feel more free to look, pick and choose. The shopping will be *cherry picking*, among brands. The personal service stores will be selling premium, customized and specialty products only. There is going to be a whole lot of addition to the services rendered at the retail outlets, viz. Credit cards, home deleveries, assorted services, etc. The first catalogue store in Bombay this year is indicator of the turn shopping is going to take. It will be almost mandatory for the producers to make the middleman a party to marketing decision making. The dealer motivation will take a turn towards non-monetary incentive. Commission will stay as important as it is, but services like shop displays, contests, general awards, cooperative advertising will form more important parts of motivation. The retailer/middleman now is recognized as an illiterate, older, conservative and a cunning person. This attitude will change as the education level is increasing and younger generation is taking over the business. They are dynamic, professional and highly forward looking. This professionalism will be seen at the retail level. The marketing principles, which are restricted to the corporate level, will also come down to retailers. The trend shows an increase in the retailer's ads. of the product than it was a decade ago. This will be on the rise. In short, retail outlet will be another profit centre of the company and the concept of Vertical Marketing System (VMS) will catch on. The conflict will not just be for trivial things like cuts and samples but at much higher policy levels. In order that a manufacturer exercises some control over the channel, it will have to make the middlemen a partner in its marketing effort.

Promotion

The aggression of promotion noticed in this decade is a continuous process. The next decade will add to the clutter. In this clutter, it is the loudest that is heard. Advertising will be the main area of thrust supported, sometimes to the same extent, by Sales Promotion techniques. The launch of the product will require a very high pitch advertising and will straightaway go for attractive offers in the form of a gift or a low price introductory offer. Though, the market is in the growth stage, the product similarity will erase all rational (quality/product based) appeals. The only rational appeal will be price or some other attachments to the product (Tie-ups).

For LIPS, Point-of-Purchase (POP) displays will play a vital role and the sellers will vie for any space. With more departmental store coming up and self-service catching up, POP display is what would be sought. For the large stores, the seller itself will try to find space. In case of small retailers, it will be the wholesalers who will be responsible for it. They will appoint *mercenaries* to snatch space from competitors. *Merchantising*[7] will be the in-thing.

For HIPS (High Involvement Products) the trend will be more personalized marketing. With EuroClean showing the path it is expected that all others will follow suit. Tele-marketing is one area which might also be a new technique tried by several marketers.

In the rural areas, hoardings and wall paintings will continue to be the leading media. TV will be the other medium used. But, the need to gather more information will invite the use of print media too. The breaks, however, will be provided by Exhibition and Fairs. These will also be a common scene in the urban areas, particularly for industrial and household goods.

Industrial advertising will be more Corporate Image Building, mostly through social and ecological concerns shown by the companies. This is done in order to get an umberella under which many diversified products could be successfully launched. Although ITC is an example to the contrary, it will be rare. Such diversification will mainly be through bids of take overs. The newer areas will be left to a new company. It will be much glamorous than most of the consumer product ads.

With the USP being lost, the consumer ads. will tend to be either abstract or comparative. The comparison may not be direct. In most of the ads., household scene will prevail over others. The use of children is another factor being an important base.

The Hindustani Ads (Vernaculars written in English) is now-a-days proving effective (Binnies, Go-Cool, Vicks, etc). It is difficult to say if this pattern will be all through the decade, but it will stay at least for a while.

Market Structure

This is an era of market consolidation. A real warfare time. The number of producers in an industry will tend to stabilise to major 20/25. Small enterpreneurs will be catering only to regional or some corners of the market. They will be seen more in rural areas trying to break into urban areas. Nirma phenomenon may not be repeated. The industrial growth will also not be as fast as seen in the last decade, where everybody thought of making it big without much thought given to marketing strategies. This is all past. A new entrant to the business will have to perfect all his weapons before a launch. A product-based launch may be extinct. Marketing will be more consumer-based with an added social concern. The companies which flourished in the last decade on the basis of technology will not find the same bait useful. The axiom "in a technology driven market, do not depend on technology for success"[8] will be followed by all leading and successful enterpreneurs.

Government policy towards industry will continue to have an open look with emphasis on indigenization, small sector and rural areas. The implementation of customer protection rules will be much stricter. The consumer becoming more aware of its rights, the consumer protection agencies will be functioning at their best. *Caveat Emptor* will be there in true sense and will make way for *Caveat Vendor*.

Conclusions

1990s, the pre-runner to the 21st Century, will be a different decade than the last. The changes may not be as outward as inward. The change will be in the philosophy or the approach of the enterpreneurs.

Apparently, the market will look like the same with the major changes being crowding of HIPS and impulse buying. But the strategies will be more penetrative and more adjusting to the competition. Technology not being a major weapon, the shift will be on to marketing, i.e., vie for a place in the mind of the customers. The marketer will have to have a very effective Marketing Information System to give more accurate, precise and detailed information about the product. The offer, in particular with HIPs, will be made as personal as possible. *Maxi-Marketing* will have to be followed. They will have to get the best out of their marketing efforts. It will also require better coordination of marketing and production department, as well as others. The decisions will have to be taken faster.

Due to impulse buying, ads. and packages will be used maximally. Brands, and not the product, will have to be positioned. Price will have to be used very strategically, since a low price may not always be an attractor. But, the non-price strategies will attract more and more customers. In any case, it will be difficult to predict the results as consumers can no way be towed. They will be more enlightened about desires and rights and will always look for a better offer, ready to switch. In short, it can be said that we have entered not into a market place but into an arena in 1990s. Some of the things that a marketer will have to bear in mind while designing a strategy may be:

1. Market pull, not the technology push, will fetch results.
2. Because technological exclusivity does not last, wonder products can not stay new life long.
3. When technology drives competition, you can not compete on technology. Nor can you count on technology to know what customers need and want.

4. Quality and prestige alone can not defend a market.
5. Products are to be considered as product portfolios.
6. It is not enough to be the right product - be the right firm with a right product at a right time.
7. There should be reduction in the product planning and development time.
8. The product development cycle has to be used strategically.
9. Development will be achieved through segmentation and concentration.
10. Market concentration to be increased by broadening market coverage.
11. Determination of sales potential is by market and not by capacity.
12. A large market position is not a strength - it is an opportunity and a threat.
13. Manage for the markets - not for the owners.
14. Get out of office and talk to the market.
15. Market is not responsible for your failure.
16. The market share has to be defended by providing superb service.
17. The product has to be into the consumer's hand as quickly as possible.
18. Do not just stand there, do something.

NOTES AND REFERENCES

1. Mukunda Das, V., "Consumer Issues in Development: A Perspective in Studying Rural Consumers", Paper presented at the First Interna-

tional Conference on Marketing and Development, Istambul, 1987.

2. Khanna, M.K., "The Changing Advertising Scene", Proceeding of the Advertising Seminar Organised by Deccan Herald, Bangalore, 1987, p. 3.

3. A Rubber Type Market is what journalists wish they had when a favourite headline fails to fit into the allotted space. The market is identified by the fact that, when all the shares of the producers, as reported by them, is added together, comes to considerably more than 100%.

4. Heller, R., *The Naked Market : Methods for the 1980s*, Sidgwick and Jackson, London, 1985, p. 32.

5. Walter Vieira, "Emerging Market For The Very Riches", *Business World*. Nov. 9-22, 1987, p. 32.

6. Heller, R., op. cit., p. 101.

7. Merchantising is a process of convincing and helping the merchants (retailers) to display a particular brand(s), in which the merchantiser deals, on the shelf or/and other POP display materials regarding that brand.

8. "Competing Beyond Technology", *Harvard Business Review*, Nov-Dec., 1989, p. 93.

3

Towards New Horizons in Marketing

KHOKAN MOOKERJI

In this paper Mr. Mookerji, a top marketing executive of the country, has dealt with new horizons of marketing in India. He has discussed in detail the major marketing trends and implications and has suggested the key issues and tasks for marketing during the 1990s. He has touched upon the macro trends such as the attitudinal changes, demographics, psychographics and communication and visualizes a movement from mass marketing to segmented marketing to niche marketing to one-to-one marketing. According to the author, the 1990s will also witness an increase in the proportion of experimental consumers i.e. consumers who are more innovative and amenable to new products and ideas. The teenagers and children will play a decisive role in making buying decisions. The increasing westernisation and internationalisation will influence the Indian marketing scene. Consumer expectation and demand for quality, safety and hygiene will continue to increase. Among other things Mr. Mookerji visualizes an expanding market for traditional consumer products as well as products which boost agricultural yields in the rural sector. Towards the end of this paper, the author foresees a diminishing dealer-retailer loyalty with increased competition amongst products, trade associations acquiring more and more bargaining power and the distribution infrastructure becoming increasingly sophisticated. Finally, he contends that Kotler's additional Ps viz. Power and Public Relations will be deployed increasingly to woo and win the Indian consumer in the years to come.

— *EDITORS*

IN the earlier decades of the present century, marketing

was considered wasteful and superfluous, especially in developing countries, which were characterised by shortages and demand management, rather than surpluses and demand promotion. Indeed, marketing in India was an imported concept and was perceived as an unfair weapon employed by multinationals for promotion of powerful foreign brand names. Marketing was also dismissed as a primarily urban activity catering to the affluent customers. Even in the 60's and 70's marketing men in India had to constantly crusade about the changed role of marketing in the context of the changing economic and social environment in India. Surely, a single decade - the 1980's - with burgeoning competition - left very little doubt about the importance of marketing in an emerging buyers market.

To cap it all, an ever-increasing phenomenon of *Globalisation* of markets, brought home the message that with increased exposure to the world-at-large, this trend will gather greater momentum, supported by massive promotional and marketing inputs which are required of world products. In this paper I propose to confine my horizons to the decade of the 90's. With Toffler's Future Shock becoming harsh reality in many areas, I dare not do crystal ball gazing beyond 2000 AD. Secondly, I will deal with marketing horizons in the Indian context and I will now proceed to enumerate some of the major marketing trends and implications it has for organisations. I will close by suggesting what might be the key issues and tasks for marketing in this decade.

Changes in the Indian Context

Though we are witnessing a sweep of ideas and conveniences from the developed countries, the very thought of change to the average Indian is rather intriguing as the concept of timelessness has been an inherent part of the Indian psyche. Also, when trend watching and predicting changes in direction, one must remember that the converse of any statement you make about a particular aspect, can be equally applicable in a country of contrasts like India. Indeed, India is an enigma. On one hand, we are the ninth largest industrial power and yet the eleventh poorest nation, in per capita terms. From possessing the third largest pool of scientific and technical manpower, we will have the dubious distinction of having the largest number of illiterates and unemployed/under-employed in the world, by 2000 AD. On one hand, we possess formidable nuclear capability and on the other, we struggle with basic metallurgy to produce a needle of consistent quality. Whatever horizons we will paint, we must remember the enduring reality of the two Indias. Witness the staggering array of contradictions. Metropolitan and urban India presents a picture of shaven check by stubby jowl - of an affluent minority with hedonistic lifestyles, co-existing with grinding poverty. Rural India possesses its own mosaic of light and shade. We witness contradictions, with consumers happily using an eclectic mix of products of Western and Indian ethos. So you have an interesting class, with a hybrid lifestyle which supports Paan Masala and Saafari suits, Silk Churidar Kurta and Benson & Hedges cigarettes. In rural India a minority of farmers holding nearly 60% of the cultivated area and accounting for nearly 40% of the consumer goods expenditure, contrast with the majority of *have-nots*.

Macro Trends and Implications

Attitudinal Changes

We are witnessing major attitudinal and life style changes, the phenomena being the movement of urban Indian consumers from Philosophical to Pragmatic, from Traditional to Contemporary and from Indian to Western.

Demographics

India's population shall increase from a current level of

837 million to nearly a 1000 million by 2000 AD. Excluding 300 million below the poverty line and keeping nearly an equal number theoretically outside our universe, we are still looking at an universe of approximately 180 million middle class which could well be in the region of 300 million by 2000 AD. The urbanisation phenomenon will continue with approximately 33% of the total population living in urban India in 2000 AD.

Dual/Multi-Income families will continue to grow as will nuclear families inviting greater freedom to choose and buy *individual* products. Thus there will be multi-product penetration in homes both quality and affordable products as also increase in household products and consumer durables. Higher aggregate incomes will throw up newer opportunities and ideas of new products and services resulting in the increase of *hi-tech* and luxury products, entertainment, vehicles, durables, travel, etc.

A Younger India - 70% of the population - will be below the age of 40 years. This will throw up vast areas of opportunity in products and services.

Changing Marketing Structure

Marketing analysis see a multi-tiered marketing structure which could be classified as teenagers, young adults, young marrieds with children, young marrieds both working, the forty plus and the growing rural rich. The broader implication being the movement from mass marketing to segmented marketing to niche marketing to one-to-one marketing, with products and appeals tailored to individual segments.

Psychographics

Changes in attitudes, habits and life-style are occuring. This results in large number of experimental consumers who are more innovative and amenable to new products and ideas. This throws up opportunities for *high-tech* products, durables and novelties, which appeal to buyers with an open attitude.

Increasing westernisation and *Internationalisation* is apparent. The West continues to exert its influence on India as do other international trends emerging from Japan, Pacific Rim countries, etc. This will have an inevitable impact in spawning a vast array of consumer durables, non-durables, and services, from automated transport and office equipment to home computers and ready-to-eat-ready-to-serve foods, fun foods, new entertainment vehicles, etc. International influences will also evoke demand for international travel. For example, today over 2 million Indians travel abroad annually and holiday habits have altered from going home to parents and relatives, to sightseeing and relaxation trips and special interest holidays like trekking, wildlife etc.

The Behaviour of Urban Consumer

The urban consumer is becoming increasingly cosmopolitan. This is resulting in greater acceptance of regional cultures, being manifested through increasing popularity of regional cuisines (e.g., Dosas & Channa/Bhatura), clothing, designs and artifacts across the country.

Growing Liberalisation

The disintegration of joint families and concurrent emergence of nuclear families has witnessed a new-found *freedom* in urban metropolitan society. This has resulted in a wider range of personal choice and home entertainment products, and the wider use of products like liquor and cigarettes at home. Another important implication of liberalisation could be shifting sources in terms of decision-making and influence. Whilst the wife/mother has already been established as an important source of authority, both teenagers and children are becoming new sources of influence with its attendant demands on manufacturers to fashion products and communication to these target groups. Maggi Noodles and Rasna are cases in point.

The Noveau Rich

At the higher income levels, we witness a new need-driven society from what was earlier a want-driven one. The more affluent consumer has become more acquisitive with the consequent demand for goods and services spanning durables, consumables, entertainment and food products. In particular, the increasing number of noveau rich are bound to seek greater upward mobility through status symbols and conspicuous consumptions. After all, a parallel economy generating Rs. 40,000 crores will have to find new avenues through which the newly-affluent discover greater material and emotional satisfaction. The means for such satisfaction range from greater demand for boarding schools, club memberships of the 'right kind', to designer-furniture, designer-wear etc. all of which aid in making the noveau rich the modern aristocrat in India. In what was essentially a caste-ridden society, such status symbols will wear down old caste labels. Hence, Levis, Crocodile, Wranglers and Puma have their own role to play.

The Changing India Woman

Growth in education, media influence, ever growing number of working women is resulting in a 'quiet revolution' in large segments of the Indian women. Today we have psychographic descridators beyond the traditional woman. The emerging Indian woman has been classified with labels like 'The Reactionary', 'The Self-Assumed', 'Confident' and 'The Health Conscious'. This has two main implications. The working woman is throwing up newer and increasing demands for personal and convenience products. Personal products range from clothing and footwear to personal care and *appearance* products of a bewildering variety. Convenience goods - mainly household items - which run the gamut from instant mixes to pressure cooker and mixies will inevitably become an integral part of middle class

India's homes. The second major implication is the need for deeper and continuing study of this major decision maker and influencer segment. Much more insights will be required to get a clearer picture of this emerging segment — their needs, activities, interests, opinions and indeed in aspects like her relationships, self-perceptions and openess to change. This will have an impact on the need for product innovation and formulations, to fashioning new areas of communication focus and new elements of persuasion.

Communication

Emergence of new communication vehicles (TV, Video, etc.), increase in domestic and foreign travel, growth on inbound tourism and influence of Indians working abroad have opened windows to the world. This has kindled new wants and desires. On one hand, there is a new generation who have the aspiration and the willingness to work towards obtaining the better things of life. Yet one vehicle alone, viz. TV, will expose two thirds of the population who will thus be exposed to the communication revolution. However, the majority will not have the means of fulfilling the newly aroused needs. Hence, we have to be very cognizent of the frightening possibilities of people with champagne thirsts and Campa Cola purses.

There is both a media boom and proliferation leading to escalating advertising spends and increasing noise levels. From a current level of Rs. 1000 crores the industry is projected to record a spend level of Rs. 2500 crores by 2000 AD. Press will continue to be the dominant medium accounting for more than 50% of the spend by 2000 AD, though the level is likely to reduce from its current level of 60%. TV could claim a quarter of the advertising spend by 2000 AD, with commercial time going up from its current level of 25%.

Other audio-visual like videos will continue to expand in scope and size with video shops and parlours proliferating from its current level of 1 lakh each and the ever escalating annual increase of VCRs from its current level of 44000 sets. Indeed with increase in literacy, the magazine and newspaper growth will continue with more specialist magazines on the increase.

Communications content will increasingly use the vernacular idiom. Firstly, the new found success of indigenous brands (e.g. Nirma, Lijjat, Vicco, Rasana, Paan Parag) and the success of indigenised appeals like *Khatak* and *Khich Khich* will further accelerate the "Indianisation of English. Equally, with communication to rural areas becoming more important a new stream of creative thinking in vernacular, must per force emerge.

Other Factors

Expanding City Limits and Increasing Time Pressures

Expanding city limits and increasing time pressures will greatly enhance the demand for household and convenience products. The escalation in consumer durable like refrigerators and mixies to washing machines will continue to be supported by higher aggregate and per capita incomes. The current refrigerator population of 9.6 lakhs, has trebled in a seven year period.

Another major fall out of this trend will be the sustained explosion in automated transport. Thus LCVs (45,000), Jeeps (35,000), trucks, buses (70,000) scooters (7.3 lakhs), motor cycles (4.1 lakhs) and cars (1.6 lakhs) will witness continued escalation of their production volumes.

The implications to manufacturers and marketers will be to constantly apply themselves to product innovation, produce quality, and affordable products ranging from transportation and home appliances to instant shoe shine and instant foods.

Health

Health consciousness is on the increase, particularly in urban India and amongst the more affluent sections, currently. This throws up new opportunities in health related products from gymnasia and saunas to jogging shoes/wear and exercise aids. Equally, new demand areas will be on the increase for ingestible health products, ranging from preventives like garlic pearls and other nature-sourced products to low calorie health foods (both packed and fresh), sugar substitutes and diet colas.

Government thrust on health-care will create a new awareness and opportunities for pharmaceutical companies and those dealing with health-related products.

Savings Rate

High inflation in land and building prices and spiralling cost is rendering them out-of-reach for a large segment. Consequently the high savings rate (20-22%) is more prone to be expanded on consumer durables, entertainment products etc.

Consumerism

With increasing education and media exposure, consumer demand for quality, safety and hygiene will continue to escalate. Significant steps have been taken through a spate of consumer-protection legislation, emergence of external pressure groups, etc.

Service Industry

The service industry will continue to record significant growth as in other parts of the world. There will be far greater competitiveness in sectors of banking, financial services, tourism, hotels and catering, consultancy services and other packaged services like janitoring and medicare.

Rural Marketing

With approximately 70% of the population still resident in rural areas and with 40% of our GDP emanating from agriculture, the rural market offers vast scope. Today we have 93 million consumers classified as the rural middle class. Rural prosperity will be further fuelled through government policies which has directed that half of the resources be available for rural development. Add to this the other source of purchasing capacity assured/support prices, remittances flowing from abroad, industry dispersal into backward areas. We are, therefore, seeing a vast market for traditional consumer products as well as products boosting agricultural yields.

Trade Channels

The distribution infrastructure is becoming increasingly sophisticated in terms of providing convenience, comfort and shelf appeal in the large cities. Additionally, time pressures will impinge on the recommendatory role of the urban retailer. Hence the need to create brands which rely less on trade push and more on consumer pull.

There will be diminishing dealer/retailer loyalty with increased competition amongst products.

Trade associations are being rolled out, within specified industry groups, particularly in cities. Such associations muster formidable bargaining power.

Megamarketing forces — with increased marketing competition, Kotler's additional Ps (Power and Public Relations) will be increasingly deployed to woo and win the consumers.

4

Consumerism : Challenges and Tasks for 90s

S. C. SAHOO

The Indian consumer is no more a pawn in the hands of the seller, claims Dr. Sahoo in this article and states that consumerism in India has arrived and is growing rapidly. The reasons for this phenomenon are the quality consciousness and the awareness caused by the media boom. The author gives examples to support it. He then goes on to suggest the tasks that lie ahead for the marketer and concludes the article on the note that there is a foreseen change from Let Buyer Be Aware to Let Seller Be Aware.

— *EDITORS*

DRUCKER once said, there is only one valid definition of business purpose: to create a customer.[1] And the first law of marketing is don't sell what you happen to make, make what the consumer wants to buy. Thus the entire philosophy of marketing centres around consumer and hence the modern marketing is called consumer-oriented marketing. With the array of changes in information technology and changing governmental regulation the marketers in the decades to come have to be more conscious of their obligations to the consuming public. Their questionable practices have provoked a sustained consumer movement. With this, an attempt is made to trace the causes of growing consumerism, some evidences of growing consumerism and to evolve the tasks and programmes for the Indian marketers for the 1990s.

Growing Consumerism : Causes

Consumerism or consumer movement is a social movement. It stands for organised efforts of consumers seeking redress, restitution and remedy for the dissatisfaction they have accumulated in the acquisition of their standard of living.[2] In USA greater education and affluence of the buyers, better communication, mass marketing and above all, the failure of business to implement the marketing concept resulted in the concept *consumerism* in the 1960s. The watchword for this new militant mood among the American consumers, according to Mrs. Virginia H. Knauer, Special Assistant to the President for Consumer Affairs was simply let the seller beware, in comparison with the age old *caveat emptor* i.e. let the buyer beware.[3] Again, the influential writings by John Kenneth Galbraith, Vance Packard and Rachel Carson accused big business of wasteful and manipulative prices. John Kennedy's Presidential Message of 1962 declared that consumers had the right to safety, to be informed, to choose, and to be heard. Congressional investigations of certain industries proved embarassing and finally, Ralph Nader appeared on the scene to crystalize many of the issues. In course of time, many private consumer organizations have emerged and several pieces of consumer legislation have been passed in the USA.[4] There was adequate production and distribution of essential as well as luxury products. The objectives of consumerism under these circumstances were to seek more information about the merits of competing products and services, and to represent the collective views of consumers in order to influence the producers. The movement by now has acquired international character, with much strength in Scandinavia, France, Germany and Japan. It has also got underway in India.

The consumer movement in India is in its infancy and is largely confined to metropolitan cities like Bombay, Ahmedabad, Hyderabad, etc. It was in April 1966, that nine housewives and social workers got together and formed the

Consumer Guidance Society of India (CGSI)to protect the consumer's interest.[5] This may be said to be the origin of consumerism in India. The shortage of essential products and the inflation of early 1973-74 encouraged the consumer movement. The movement has been boosted up by several factors.

The rising prices of goods and services have created in consumers an attitude to expect better quality and if it is not forthcoming creates dissatisfaction among them. Further, the inflationary tendency prevailing in recent times has made purchasing more difficult. Hence the consumers have become more conscious of their spending as well as of rights.

A large variety of products in the market place has created product complexity. This complexity has been encouraged by new and changing technology. This makes the consumer to expect perfect products. Similarly, the advertising making exaggerated claims about the products creates an expectation of better performance of products.

The spread of education coupled with rising incomes of the people has also been responsible for the intensification of the movement.

The legislations[6] intended to protect the consumers' interest in the country has created an awareness among the consumers about their rights and remedies available to them. Particularly the enactment of the Consumer Protection Act, 1986 (COPRA) has provided a real impetus to the movement. The consumer, who had been relegated to the sidelines has been increasingly coming to occupy centre-stage. The speedy compensations granted by different forums have convinced the consumer of the efficacy of quasi-judicial machinery (under COPRA) and strengthened his confidence which is likely to make him more assertive. This, Ramkrishna Bajaj observes, is bound to give a much-needed boost to the consumer movement in days to come.[7]

An increasing awareness among the public regarding

various social problems and greater social responsibilities of the business has also contributed substantially to the consumer movement in India. Above all, the idea that the consumer is the king in the market place has in reality been largely discarded and in its place the idea that he is a pawn in the hands of the businessman is a major driving force of consumer movement.

As mentioned earlier, the formation of CGSI in 1966 was the starting point of consumer movement in India. Today it has over 2,500 members and five branches — at Hyderabad, Dandeli, Pune, Kottayam and Trichur. It is gratifying to note that over the years, CGSI has excelled itself in the publicising of test conducted by it on various products edible and electric. Among other such notable organisations responsible for promoting consumerism are Consumer Education and Research Centre (CERC) at Ahmedabad, Voluntary Organisation in the Interest of Consumer Education (VOICE), Indian Federation of Consumer Organisations (IFCO) and the Common Cause, New Delhi and Council for Fair Business Practices (CPBP), Bombay.

Growing Consumerism : Some Evidences

That the consumer is the king or that there is growing consumerism in India can be seen from some of the evidences cited here.

Ranbaxy Laboratories, a reputed company in the pharmaceuticals industry failed to make any dent in the toiletries market. Its consumer toiletries under the brand name *Naturelle* could not carve a sustainable niche. Again, Eskayef, a much envied drug company's extension into consumer toiletries also turned into a fiasco when its brand named *Superfresh* could not gain consumer acceptance. Burroughs Welcome — a successful drug company's venture into the consumer toiletries failed to take off at the very introductory stage. There are many such instances where products — new or modified have failed due to consumer's non-acceptance. What do all these reveal? These are nothing but indications to the manufacturers that they can no more manufacture anything and everything they like and make the consumers buy the same. That time is fast disappearing.

To cite a few more, a public interest petition was filed against Indian Airlines before the National Commission to highlight inadequate maintenance and over-use of IA aircraft which had led to serious safety hazards. This alongwith another petition against the Delhi Electric Supply Undertaking (DESU) was filed by Common Cause, an all-India consumer protection group, with the National Commission on Consumer Disputes Redressal (NCCDR).[8] The Common Cause Director, Mr. H.D. Shourie contended that the complaint against IA assumed significance in light of the Ahmedabad crash. In the other petition against DESU it was pointed out that in certain areas of Delhi consumers had not received bills for six to twelve months which obviously caused ways and means problems to the DESU necessitating in raising loans leading to increase in tariff.

Coming to Orissa, an economically less developed State the State Level Commission in pursuance with the provision of the Consumer Protection Act, 1986 was constituted in January 1989. Presently out of 13 districts 11 have already formed district forums for the redressal of consumer complaints. In one case the Orissa Consumers Federation filed a complaint regarding the non-supply of required medicines to the patients and about poor maintenance of toilets, etc. in the S.C.B. Medical College Hospital, Cuttack. The Commission intervened and directed the authorities concerned for immediate compliance which was acted upon. A petition was also filed against the Orissa State Electricity Board (OSEB) alleging irregular supply of power, irregular billing and unusual delay in giving new connections to various applicants. Even disconnection of lines without due notice was brought to the knowledge of the Commission. The Commission directed the Board to rectify these irregularities to avoid harrassment to the consumers. Again, a petition containing similar complaints was filed against the Telephones Department. The authorities of the department confessed before the Commission their faults and assured the latter that in future such mistakes will not occur. Even the people of Orissa went to the extent of bringing to the notice of the Commission the unusual delay in the publication of results by the Council of Higher Secondary Education, Orissa. Within a period of about one year of its functioning as many as 75 cases have been disposed of by the Commission in Orissa.[9] These are all clear evidences of the fact that consumerism has acquired momentum and shall pose a challenge to the industry and trade in the days to come.

Many States and Union Territories have already constituted the State Level Commissions and also district forums for a speedy redressal of consumer grievances. But they are now confronted with difficulties such as lack of adequate funds, infrastructural facilities and so on. It is hoped, in course of time such difficulties shall be overcome and the functioning of such consumer courts will be more efficient and effective in the larger interest of the poorly equipped consuming public.

Tasks Ahead

Many enlightened and progressive managements are alive to their responsibilities to the society in general. They provide satisfactory after-sale service, hear consumer complaints and replace the product or offer free maintenance and repair. Some of them have recognised the need for guaranteed performance of their products. Price tags and informative labels are being appended for the information of the consumer. They are also undertaking truthful advertising and are avoiding misleading appeals. They know that the business interest and consumerism both aim at the protection of the consumer at the market place. They are, therefore, taking positive steps to safeguard the consumer interest by adopting consumer-oriented marketing. More and more companies are now creating a consumers affairs cell/department. A few companies in India such as Bajaj Electricals, State Bank of India and the like have also started forming consumer conferences in order to deal with consumer complaints.

As regards the Government regulation through legislation, it is observed that it is not enough to enact consumer legislations but their enforcement both in letter and spirit is more important. However, experience shows that enforcement is awfully ineffective mainly due to plethora of laws, lack of and paucity of proper personnel, inefficient organisation, red tapism and large-scale corruption. But there will be no need for governmental regulation if the businessmen maintain high social and moral values, and practise self-regulation and self-discipline. Now the question is what should be the tasks and programmes for the companies to respond to the growing consumerism?

First, the starting point of a company programme to respond to consumerism is to establish and maintain an effective and efficient consumer communication system. Because until recently, the seller's market had dulled the business community's sense of urgency about attending to consumer grievances. As a result, a communication gap had developed between the consumer on the one hand, and the manufacturer and dealer on the other. The practice of creating consumer affairs department/consumer relations department is spreading in the developed countries. It indicates corporate acceptance of social responsibility. It also points out recognition of consumer's bill of rights. Indian companies should establish and follow such practices and provide distributive justice to Indian consumers. A sound consumer communication system will serve as listening post for consumer inquiries and complaints and to see that they are properly answered. In fact, such an effort will be almost like the concept of an *ombudsman* (Lokayukta). A consumers affairs department will provide a better two-way communication with consumer. This department will represent and advocate for the consumer interests when policies and programmes are being formulated. It will provide an independent appraisal of the company's marketing programme. Thus, consumers can indirectly participate in the policy-making process through this department. Besides, the department will develop and operate an information system generating more and more information to consumers. It can publish instructional booklets on the use and care of the company's products.

Consumer conferences may be organised at the instance of the companies to deal with consumer complaints and also to facilitate an interaction between the consumers and the companies. Such conferences are also a part of the total communication system. Already a few companies in India such as Bajaj Electricals, State Bank of India and Life Insurance Corporation of India have started this practice. It is suggested that others should also adopt this soon.

In the light of increased government efforts to prosecute illegalities and the role of the press to publicize unethical business practices, a useful code of ethics should be developed and its development should be the major concern of marketers in the 1990s. Companies should conduct periodic seminars in ethics for their marketing executives enabling them to discuss the social and ethical dimensions of strategic marketing decisions.

No doubt the consumer-oriented legislations are meant to protect the interest of consumers still the fruits of these are yet to reach the consumers particularly in the tribal and rural areas of the country. It is still felt that the government have to play the catalyst role in providing real protection to the consumer especially in a developing country like ours till awareness is generated and sustained. The businessmen should also bear in mind that it is high time that they should take positive action tc demonstrate their interest in more general accord with consumer's needs and wants, and offer full consumer satisfaction. Then only the business can prosper and consumers can be assured equity and justice in the market place. The businessmen must be aware of the present mood of the society and act accordingly.

Thus multi-pronged efforts are required for the success of consumer movement and for effective implementation of the various legislations as well.

NOTES AND REFERENCES

1. Drucker, Peter F. *The Practice of Management*, Allied Publishers Private Ltd., N. Delhi, 1988, p. 37.

2. Buskirk, R.H. and James T. Rothe, "Consumerism - An Interpretation", *Journal of Marketing*, Vol. 34, October, 1979, p. 62.

   In the Indian context the meaning of consumerism given by Philip Kotler is worth noting. He says, it is an organized movement of citizens and government to strengthen the rights and power of the buyers in relation to sellers.
   — *Marketing Management*, Prentice-Hall of India, N. Delhi, 1988, p. 142.

3. "The Consumer Revolution", *US News and World Report*, Vol, LXVII, August 25, 1969, pp. 43-46.

4. See *Exhibit – I, U.S. Legislations on Consumer Protection.*

5. Davar, R.S. *Modern Marketing Management*, Crown Publishing House, Bombay, 1986, p. 44.

6. See *Exhibit – II, Indian Legislations on Consumer Protection.*

7. Bajaj, Ramakrishna, "New Challenge Before Industry", *The Times of India*, N. Delhi, May 23, 1990, p. 13.

8. *The Prajatantra* (Oriya Daily) Cuttack, January 24, 1990.

EXHIBIT – I

U.S. Legislations On Consumer Protection

1. Sherman Antitrust Act, 1890,
2. Federal Food and Drug Act, 1906
3. Meat Inspection Act, 1906,
4. Clayton Act, 1914,
5. Antimerger Act, 1950,
6. Automobile Information Disclosure Act, 1958,
7. National Traffic and Safety Act, 1958,
8. Fair Packaging and Labeling Act, 1966,
9. Child Protection Act, 1966,
10. Truth-in-Lending Act, 1968,
11. Federal Cigarette Labeling and Advertising Act, 1967,
12. National Environment Policy Act, 1969
13. Consumer Product Safety Act, 1972,
14. Consumer Goods Pricing Act, 1975,
15. Fair Debt Collection Practice Act, 1978.

EXHIBIT – II

Indian Legislations on Consumer Protection

1. The Drugs and Cosmetics Act, 1940,
2. The Drugs and Magic Remedies (Objectionable Advertisement) Act, 1954,
3. The Prevention of Food (Adulteration) Act, 1954.
4. The Essential Commodies Act, 1955,
5. The Standards of Weights and Measures Act, 1955.
6. The Trade and Merchandise Act, 1958.
7. The Essential Services Maintenance Act, 1958.
8. The Monopolies and Restrictive Trade Practices Act, 1969.

9. The Packaged Commodities Order 1975.
10. The Household Electrical Appliances (Quality Control) Order, 1976.
11. The Prevention of Black Marketing and Maintenance of Supplies of Essential Commodities Act, 1980.
12. The Bureau of Indian Standards Act, 1986.
13. The Consumer Protection Act, 1986.

5

The Growth and Challenges of Rural Market

S.K. PATRO

The Indian rural market is vast and expanding. The manufacturers particularly of consumer products have started tapping this market. Prof. Patro in this paper has pointed out the how and why of the growth of rural market. While analysing the emerging scenario of the rural market the author suggests to take note of institutional reforms, increased investment in rural development, etc. He opines that no uniform strategy can be adopted to market goods to all segments of the rural market which are varied in nature. Prof. Patro has recommended for a region-wise study of various marketing parameters and for an analysis of rural consuming system as essentials.

— *EDITORS*

As a result of the country's successive Five Year Plans since the 1950s, agricultural productivity has improved significantly. India is no longer a country reeling under acute food shortages. Now it is self-sufficient in its food grain requirements to feed the second largest populated country. Without doubt this has given a new impetus to India's rural economy. Year by year more and more areas of cultivable land are provided with irrigation facilities. Consolidation of land in many a states have also brought the economies of large scale cultivation. The technological innovations in developing hybrid seeds and using efficient agricultural implements have contributed to higher productivity, thereby providing higher purchasing power in the hands of the rural people.

The gross domestic product (GDP) from agriculture is 32 per cent and that of the industrial sector is 22 per cent. Of this one-third of the industrial sector's contribution is directly related to inputs into the agricultural sector. Although the contribution of primary sector to the national income is decreasing, in order to provide gainful employment to the rural mass the government is giving priority to rural and agricultural investments. In the eighth Five-Year Plan the Government has decided to have 50 per cent of the total outlay for the agricultural sector. In the budget of 1990-91, the rural investment has increased by 4 per cent than the previous year's allocation. Thus government's huge investments in the various programmes and projects in the rural areas have provided employment to the rural folk which has a circulatory effect.

There is a reduction in the perceived risk of agriculture as mixed cropping systems are adopted. This has led the farmers to spend their surpluses in buying consumer durables, non-durables and efficient agricultural implements. Earlier farmers were investing the surpluses in buying additional land and cattlestock. As the risk perceived by the farmers have decreased, the demand for consumer durables and non-durables have increased.

In spite of the high rate of urban population growth the rural market offers opportunities which are vast and relatively untapped. The Indian market is larger than the market of many European countries put together. Rural India possesses its own mosaic of light and shade. The top 13% of farmers holding nearly 57% of the cultivable area and accounting for nearly 40% of the consumer goods expenditures, contrasted with the majority of *'have-nots'*. Of late Government's specific area and specific community programmes have benefitted the lower segments of the society and have given purchasing power to them.

A thorough analysis of urban *vis-a-vis* rural population

will show that the style of living, the number of gadgets used are strikingly different even in case of the segments of population with the same purchasing power. It is so because the exposure of the urban population to the winds of change is larger than that of a rural society. A rural society, conservative in its modes and standards, acts as a great wall obstructing the new ideas and advocations. But gradually the rural society has shed its conservative outlook. One will be pleasantly surprised to see many rural people now asking for branded goods and postponing their purchases until they get their preferred items. No longer we can assume that rural people settle for cheaper and low quality goods. The recent studies show that they are brand loyal and in an environment where there is a lack of adequate information, the buyers' preference for branded goods just explains their logical behaviour of risk reduction.

The success of green revolution is mostly referred as a marketing wonder. The farmers have abdicated the age old practices of cultivation and have adopted the new ideas and the new tools of cultivation. Yet another example is the success of family planning in India. Here also the rural mass have been exposed to a radical new thinking of smaller is better and the results are for all to see. These examples show that the rural population is amenable to change which is opposite to the traditional thinking that they are hard-core conformists.

While analysing the emerging scenario of rural market we have to take note of the developments, such as (a) Institutional reforms (strengthening of Panchayat Raj system), (b) Increased investment in rural development (The ripple effect of this investment is likely to increase the demand for consumer durables and non-durables), (c) its heterogeneity, the socio-cultural background of different groups as strikingly different. Hence a uniform strategy cannot be adopted to market goods to all these varied segments of rural customer. Very often the marketing strategies and techniques developed in the west are applied in India as such. The urban conglomerations are to some extent similar to the western culture and values. But it is a great folly to apply the same technique to market goods to the rural consumers. The failure of some of the popular brands of the West in India manifests this only.

Hence a region-wise study of marketing parameters is necessary. A uniform strategy cannot be adopted for the whole of rural India. Here market segmentation procedures are to be used effectively as the rural market is not a single large market but it consists of a number of small market segments.

Another factor which has to be analysed in depth is the relationship between the stage of development of the village economy and the demand for consumer goods. In the first stage of development the demand for rurally produced goods is high. Here agriculture is still in the primitive stage and secondary and tertiary sectors are almost dormant. The infrastructures of these villages are also underdeveloped. As the other sectors are not developed the economic condition of the people are more of subsistence in nature. So a lack of purchasing power in the hands of the people reinforced with inaccessibility to new ideas and lack of exposure to the print and electronic media lead to a low aspiration level and they are not after the branded goods. They remain contented with the locally produced items. Hence here rural to rural transaction is predominant.

In the second stage of development agricultural activities have undergone a change from the primitive practices to the more developed methods of cultivation. Here some secondary activities like handicrafts are there. The rurally produced goods are used and at the same time there is a preference for urban consumer goods.

In the third stage of development agriculture is very well developed. In addition to the traditional cereal crops the farmers cultivate cash crops which supplements their income to a great extent. The contribution of secondary and tertiary sectors is also significant. The infrastructures like storage, communication are fairly well developed. These villages are not very far from the urban areas. Hence the interaction of these villagers with the urban population is very high.

The communications revolution is influencing both urban and rural India. Around 2/3rd of our population is exposed to the power of electronic media, specially television. Seeing is believing. It is the most powerful medium to influence the consumers. As majority of the rural consumers are exposed to this media, the marketers have got a potentially powerful tool to convert the latent needs into potent requirements. The rural folk consciously or unconsiously are imbibing modern ways of living which has led to a rise in their aspiration level.

While enlisting the opportunities of the rural market, a number of daunting problems that effect the growth of the rural market are also to be analysed. The marketing effort for manufactured consumer goods as well as agricultural inputs in rural areas is constrained by (a) high distribution cost, (b) high initial market development expenditure, (c) inability of the small retailers to carry stocks without adequate credit facility, and (d) inadequate infrastructural facilities.

In rural areas often it is not the promotion of a brand that is crucial but creating an awareness about the product class. In these situations *syndicated advertising* can bring down the market development expenditure. Here a few companies with similar product lines will collaborate collectively in creating awareness of their products and in gaining consumer preference for their products.

There are wide regional variations in the prosperity levels of districts and hence in their market potential. These need to be analysed and be understood sectorally in order to determine the methods of approaching them.

There are about 6,00,000 villages in India, 79 per cent of them with a population less than 1000. Rural consumers are also far less homogenous than their urban counterparts, and differ from region to region. The low density of population and inaccessibility makes the problem of servicing these villages individually difficult and very often uneconomical. Direct delivery of goods to even the top 1% of villages costs twice as much as servicing urban markets. Therefore, in the initial stage it will be better to concentrate only on the larger villages, mandi towns and towns with large agricultural hinterlands that act as foci for distribution. These mandi villages can become the gate ways for entry into the rural market.

India is a vast country with people of different cultural, historical and traditional backgrounds. Prosperity differs from one state to another. There is no doubt that a large number of farmers have adopted improved methods of cultivation and technical developments. What we need is greater knowledge of the scale of values of rural consumers. A farmer may possess an expensive transistor, but he may not show the same interest to such things as good clothes, good shaving systems, and costly detergent powders.

In developing economies like India, while analysing the rural markets the study of the rural consuming system* is highly relevant. In order to clearly understand the marketing implications of agrarian material prosperity in a country like India, the classified parameters of marketing environment such as economic, social or technological do not help much. In addition to these studies, the rural consuming systems analysis has to be done. The rural market which is vast but relatively untapped has thrown a big challenge to the marketers which when met will bring a new era of prosperity to the country.

---

* For details see article "India's Emerging Consumer Markets: Relevance of the Evolving Rural Consuming Systems", by Prof. V. Mukunda Das in this volume.

6

India's Emerging Consumer Markets

Relevance of the Evolving Rural Consuming Systems

V. MUKUNDA DAS

A study of the evolution of the rural consuming system is relevant in a developing economy like India. This is because of the fact that rural market is assuming greater importance day by day which, in turn, is due to improved agricultural productivity and the flow of increasingly large investments to rural sector from various sources. Prof. Das in this paper has discussed the evolution of the rural consuming system and its relevance in India. The author observes two important changes in the buying pattern of the rural consumer viz. change from more land to more consumer durables and change from locally made goods to urban consumer goods. The author has identified the facilitating factors and the critical conditions contributing to the process of evolving a rural consuming system. The marketing implications of the changes have also been scanned. Prof. Das asserts that the understanding of the process behind the evolution of the consuming systems and not the classified parameters of marketing environment - economic, social or technological - would help the Indian marketers in the days to come.

— EDITORS

A significant development over the last decade in Indian marketing milieu was the awareness of the dichotomy between urban and rural markets. Much academic attention is now focused to the studies on rural market as the urban marketing conditions have been, relatively, researched more. Because of the environmental conditions that differ *vis-a-vis* the urban and rural consumers, the impact of material prosperity generates different scenarios in the consuming system. Changes in the Indian urban consuming system were found to be more or less similar to the developed countries because of the urban ecology and system of life. However, the rural consuming system and its evolution is observed to be different. Moreover, while in terms of the size, the urban consumers constitute only 30 per cent of the Indian consumers, the rural consumers constitute about 70 per cent. Further, the rural market is assuming importance due to the rapid pace of material prosperity because of improved agricultural productivity and the flow of increasingly large investments to rural development from many sources. Therefore, it becomes relevant to understand the rural consuming systems, the direction of changes in it and identify the facilitating factors and critical conditions contributing to its evolutionary process.

While marketing studies deal in many details with the post-industrial societies of the west and their marketing environment, similar focus purely on the marketing environment of developing countries on classified parameters such as economic, social, political and technological, has become inadequate in the context of speedy developments in the agrarian sector of developing countries such as India. Nicosia and Mayer observed "the social and economic process that led to the development of western societies no longer seem to work. In particular the visibility of consumption styles in western societies both the kind and the intensity of consumption in developing societies, so that the old cycle of saving-investment-production and then consumption no longer seems applicable to these societies".[1] However, so far very little research has gone into these aspects of developing societies.

In a related context Kaynak[2] observed "Marketing

systems are not static. They evolve over a period of time and are closely associated with over all conditions in a given LDC (less developed country) and its stage of socio-economic and technological development. These marketing systems evolve as part of the overall socio-economic, cultural, and technological development of an LDC". Schultz while studying on marketing in traditional subsistence economies mentioned that "changes in the production system (of these economies) and facilities are likely to accommodate themselves to needs as they emerge"[3]. This shows that the analysis and elucidation of various elements of the marketing environment acts only as a trace of the background. On the other hand, the consuming systems emerge as a result of the continuous interaction of the socio-economic, technological and political parameters which are only individually dealt in the analysis of marketing environment. Therefore, the study of the evolution of consuming systems show the process which is more important to a marketer in a developing country like India from an operational view point. In India, the conclusions of growing rural market only focussed on the economic environmental aspect of market potential and not on how the rural consumer market is emerging.

To elucidate the two dominant shifts in consumption in India's rural consuming system an attempt has been made to outline a conceptual framework. This is expected to explain the direction of changes in the rural consuming system. In identifying the two facilitating factors and one critical condition, out of probably many, the effect of these factors in their relation to the rural consuming system has been observed and studied.

Bases of Study

The conceptual framework is based on three types of studies. First, the study on rural consumers (Das, 1986) made continuously over the last 5 years in Kaira district of

Gujarat with a view to know the factors affecting consumer choice behaviour.[4] This district is typical in terms of the prosperity in the agrarian sector and the faster pace of its occurence.[5] Districts in other parts of the country similar in terms of quicker agrarian prosperity have been documented.[6] This helped generalisations about rural India. Secondly, the studies such as NCAER on rural income and disposition also were considered for deriving certain salient features of the rural consumption. Thirdly, supporting evidence on the changes in the consumption profile were drawn from the studies on rural consumption in Gujarat (AERC) and resurveys of economic and social profiles and changes in it of selected villages. The studies by Agro Economic Research Centres (AERC) documented the quantitative differences between two periods in the consumption of items and did not go into the socio-cultural process that were instrumental in such changes in consumption. In addition, we also used Mass Observation Approach in verifying the main tenets of these studies through visits of villages in some states in India.

Direction of Change

There are two dominant changes/shifts discerned in the rural consuming system. These changes, it is to be understood, are from a pre-agrarian prosperity level to one after agrarian prosperity or rural development investments. The first change in spending is manifested in an increasing proportion of incremental income being spent for buying consumer durables from a previous state of buying more land, in the affluent segments of rural consumers. The second change is from a situation of buying locally made (mostly within the village) goods to one of buying urban made consumer goods.

Change from more Land to more Consumer Durables

The emergence of this trend has been more due to the

innate development within the rural system than the result of marketing efforts as is usually the case in the developed western countries. Needless to add that the emergence of this trend has tremendously increased the potential for consumer durables. The market for consumer durables was mostly confined to urban India till the above trend emerged. This has also been captured in the data on consumption expenditure on consumer durables (NSS). The extent of rural spending previous to agricultural prosperity have been found as lower when compared with urban.

Having now mentioned the phenomenon, let us identify the combination of interacting factors enabling this evolution in the rural consuming system. They are (a) spurt in agrarian prosperity (b) the perception of reduction in risk in agriculture (c) changes in the (conception) of ideal consumption basket. The first two factors could be stated as facilitating factors and the third as a critical condition for the evolution to take place.

(a) Spurt in Agrarian Prosperity

The spurt in agrarian prosperity had enabled the rural consumers to reach higher levels of income. This income increase was caused by technological developments inducing higher production.[7] This higher production increased income levels especially of those segments which had higher market surplus. Converted into monetary terms this spurt in agricultural income in rural India contributed to increased material base of some rural segments, and are estimated to be in a few million rupees in size. However, the incremental income could have been spent more for buying land and/or gold at an increasing rate as in the pre-prosperity days when the proportion of incremental income spent on consumer durables were almost nil. On the contrary this spurt in agrarian prosperity has induced changes in the perception of those segments of the consumers regarding consumption choices considerably.

This resulted in the change over or evolution to purchase of consumer durables, which showed a significant departure from the past in the rural consuming system.

(b) Reduction of Risk (perceived) in Agriculture

The increased productivity in agriculture changed the agricultural operations from a state of subsistence and primitivism to one commercialised. Therefore, concomitant with the increased income from agriculture was the perception among the rural consumer segments with surplus income about the reduced risk in agriculture. The perceived risk in agricultural production was found very high before the spurt in agrarian prosperity. The uncertainty in income received from agriculture because of its total dependence on natural conditions and low technology has now been changed. This has changed the 'psyche' of the segments of rural consumers resulting in, simultaneously, induced changes from buying more land/gold to consumer durables. The perception of reduced risk could generate an atmosphere for increased potential for change in the consuming system.

(c) Change in the (conception) of Ideal Consumption Basket

This is the critical condition for the direction of change in the rural consuming system. It has been stated that urban consumers in general are more impulsive in purchase decisions compared with rural consumers. Unlike the urban consumers, consumers in rural India follow a concept of ideal consumption and this concept is related and defined in the context of economic and social classes. The concept of ideal consumption is thus related to the material conditions and consumption values. Therefore, as material conditions change, changes could occur in the conception of ideal consumption. The concept of ideal consumption basket is derived by the rural consumers from the conception of desired consumption basket. Whereas the desired consumption basket is basically an individual consumer's psychological disposition the ideal consumption basket is one validated by the social norms. While the desired consumption basket is defined by individual consumers, the ideal consumption tends to be socially desirable also. Any change in income, especially when it is sudden, acts on the ideal consumption system. Therefore, depending on the change in the economic factors, individual consumers usually tend to change the ideal consumption basket. Before the agrarian prosperity, the concept of ideal consumption basket was significantly different for the rural consumer segments we are considering now. The consumption basket included land and gold as the most important elements. However, after the agrarian prosperity, the changed ideal consumption basket consists of consumer durables as important elements.

The evolution of consuming system is thus a result of a changed consumption choice. This evolution is brought in by the mutual reinforcement of the two factors as the critical condition which is shown in diagram – I. The white area in the diagram shows the mutually reinforced juncture for changed choice highlighting the evolutionary process.

Marketing Implications

The implications of this to the marketers are obvious and clear. In the context of India the marketers of consumer durables have understood the first two factors. However, they failed to understand the third, the critical condition. In the absence of this the marketing exercises were not streamlined even to try out appropriate communication programmes to influence the potential consumers. Therefore, the increased purchases of consumer durables (for example, tractors in Gujarat) were more because of the *pull* by the consuming system than any deliberately planned efforts by the marketing system.

Change from Locally made Goods to Urban Consumer Goods

One of the differences in this trend is the difference in the facilitating factors. While an economic improvement due to rural development investment contributes as a facilitating factor (instead of the low risk perception factor in the previous case) it is the influence of filtered urban consumption values that transcend the facilitating context in this trend. The two trends are shown in Box 1.

Source of Income	Purchase Effect	
	Durables	Nondurables
Agrarian	High	Low
Public Rural Development	Low	High

Whereas in the previous case of shift the segments of rural consumers having increased income due to higher agricultural productivity and market surplus (commercialised agriculture) was mainly instrumental in bringing changes in the consuming system the shift in the present case is confined to land owning segment alone. This shift in the preference and, as a result, the change in buying of branded urban consumer goods to that of locally made could even be observed among labourers employed in rural employment programmes (there are many rural employment programmes in India that take up to provide employment to rural people). This is partly because of the relatively low unit price of consumer non-durables as compared to consumer durables. From locally made coir ropes to plastic ropes manufactured in urban areas as also locally made cosmetics to urban made are some such examples of shifting preferences.

However, it should be noted that elements in the ideal

consumption basket in this case are subjected to scrutiny and therefore selectively bought because of the high social involvement associated with some of these. For example, using / buying transparent sarees by women are taboo though using polyester sarees are not objected to, in most rural areas. This phenomenon is similar to the findings of Witt and Bruce studies that showed that "products high in social involvement are those which are frequently used in the presence of other people and which have certain images which are transferred to the user".[8]

Marketing Implications

The filtering of consumption choices of individuals by rural society especially relating to personal effects, mostly coming under consumer non-durables, have high social involvement. The cultural mediation in Indian rural society is different from that of urban society. It is in this context that a good understanding of the rural consuming system and direction of change is important for the Indian marketers whose experience is mostly confined to India's urban market. Therefore, attempts to replicate such urban marketing experiences and assumptions would be inappropriate in rural India. The rural social context of the buying and usage of non-durables should be better understood. It is this social context that determines the elements in ideal consumption basket.

Conclusion

In developing economies like India the study of the evolution of rural consuming system is highly relevant, in the context of spurt in economic prosperity occuring through agricultural and rural development, because it can reveal how the consuming system adjust to such spurt in material prosperity. The facilitating context for the evolution of such consuming system is not provided by marketing efforts than through the interaction of certain relevant factors and conditions.

In order to clearly understand the marketing implications of agrarian material prosperity in a country like India, the classified parameters of marketing environment such as economic, social or technological do not help. What is required is the understanding of the process behind the evolution of rural consuming systems.

We have identified two dominant trends in India's rural consuming system and the conceptual bases of how these trends emerged. These two trends in consuming system were found in relation to consumer durables and non-durables consumption. While attempting to explain the evolution in India's rural consuming system we found that the rural market for consumer durables and non-durables generated increased potential not because of the initiative of Indian marketers but by the *pull* from the consuming system. Moreover, we found that, more in the case of non-durables than durables, the urban experience and judgement in marketing do not pay much as the group influence in society on purchase of these are stronger and complex than in urban areas.

REFERENCES

1. Francesco M. Nicosia and Robert N. Mayer, "Toward a Sociology of Consumption", *Journal of Consumer Research*, Vol. 3, September, 1976. pp. 65-75.
2. Erdener Kaynak, *Marketing in the Third World*, Praeger, New York, 1982, p. 35.
3. Schultz. T.W. (1964) *Transforming Traditional Agriculture*, Yale University Press, New Haven, Conn.
4. Mukunda Das, V (1964), "Consumer goods, flow into rural India : Evidences from some village in Gujarat", (unpublished), Institute of Rural Management, Anand, Gujarat, India.
5. Mario Rutten, "Social Profile of Agricultural Entrepreneurs : Economic Behaviour and Life style of Middle/large Farmers in Central

Gujarat", *Review of Agriculture, Economic and Political Weekly,* Vol. XXI, No. 13, 1986.

6. Bhalla G.S. and Y.K. Alagh, (1979) *Performance of Indian Agriculture : A District-wise Study,* Sterling Publishers Pvt. Ltd., New Delhi.

7. Hanumantha Rao, CH (1975), *Technological Change and Distribution of Grains in Indian Agriculture,* Institute of Economic Growth, New Delhi.

8. Robert E Witt and Grady D Bruce, "Group Influence and Brand Choice Congruence", *Journal of Marketing Research,* Vol. 9, November, 1972, pp. 440-443.

DIAGRAM - I

Facilitating Context

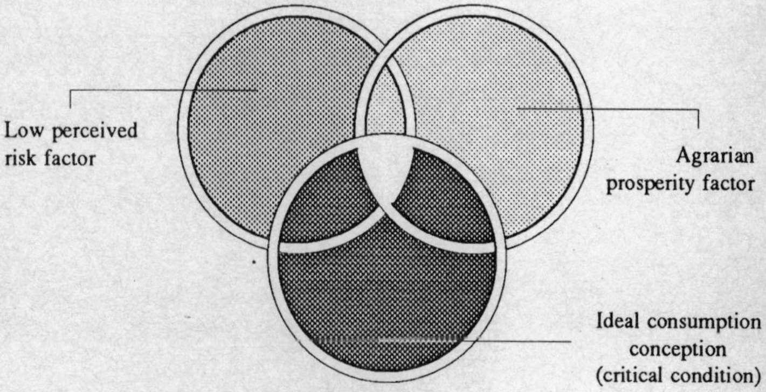

DIAGRAM - II

Facilitating Context

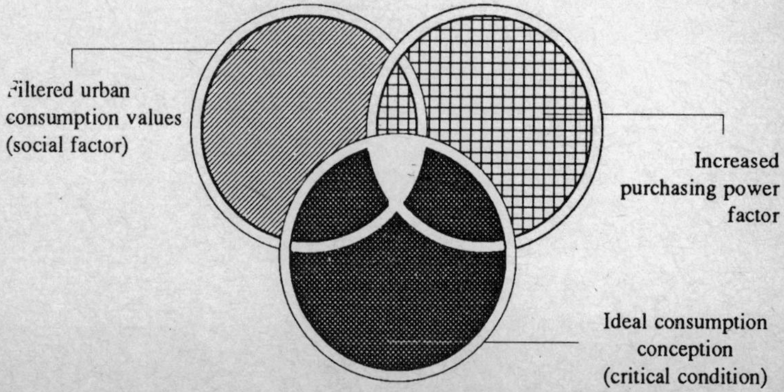

7

Emerging Trends in India's Export Markets

S. C. SAHOO

This attempt by Dr. Sahoo is in the direction of exploring the present activities and forecasting the changes that are likely to take place on India's export front. The paper highlights that the BoP scene is still far from satisfactory, though it is showing the signs of improvement. India has always been an exporter : of traditional goods, the Star products. But the challenge is in the Sunrise products which will require a clever marketing strategy to beat the competitors that will also be vying for a share.

India, indicates Dr. Sahoo, is emerging as a power in the Asian Continent and the trends show that smaller countries are approaching us with an offer of exports, particularly of consultancies & turnkey projects. India should grab this opportunity with both hands.

The author also throws light on the strategies that would be useful for achieving a progressive mode. He suggests the application of Korean formula to penetrate developed economies. India generally loses because of prices. A measure to reduce this has to be taken. Dr. Sahoo concludes with the remark that only marketing orientation can help boost India's exports.

— *EDITORS*

THE foreign exchange needs of a developing country may be met from various sources such as foreign official grants, aids and loans, private flows and exports. Of these, export earnings are the only dependable source of foreign exchange for any developing country like India. The reasons are not far to seek. First, the reliance on official grants, aids and loans means dependence of a country's developmental efforts on the whims and fancies of an outside agency as well as the vagaries of international politics. Secondly, such aids and loans carry with them high servicing charges and repayment obligations and several other stings attached to them. Finally, it is vital to export and earn foreign exchange in order to pay for the import of food, machinery, materials, and technology for economic growth. Thus in the context of the need to strive for economic development and to improve unfavourable trade balance, development of export trade and expansion of export earnings assume strategic importance. It is this crucial role of exports that calls for formulating an appropriate strategy so that the competitive strength of the country is considerably enhanced over the years.

This paper attempts to examine the current balance of payment scenario, export performance, emerging trends in the composition and direction of India's exports and the role played by the Government in export promotion to arrive at the strategies to improve the country's share in the world market.

Balance of Payment Scenario

The role of self-reliance and the need to base developments primarily on resources mobilised domestically have always been emphasised in the India's development plans. To achieve this objective and also to restrict the current account deficits to a manageable proportion has always remained an integral part of the development strategy. Unfortunately, however, Indian economy has, by and large, faced difficult balance of payments situations right from the First Plan with a few exceptional years. The key indicators presented in Table-1 give an idea of the India's balance of payment scenario.

The trade deficit averaged 3.7 per cent of GDP during the Sixth Plan. It increased to 3.7 per cent of GDP in 1985-86 due mainly to a lacklustre export performance, declined in 1986-87 to 3.2 per cent of GDP both on account of better export performance and further declined to 2.8 per cent of GDP in 1987-88 and to 2.3 per cent in 1988-89 mainly due to good growth in exports.[1] Net earnings on invisibles account fell from an average of 2.1 per cent during the Sixth Plan to 1.2 per cent of GDP in 1985-86 and 1986-87 and further to 0.9 per cent of GDP in 1987-88 reflecting both a rise in interest payments on external loans and credits, and declining importance of private transfers.[2] However, the same increased to 1.1 per cent of GDP in 1988-89. As a consequence of these trends in trade and invisible accounts, the current account deficit rose sharply from an average of 1.5 of GDP in the Sixth Plan to 2.5 per cent in 1985-86. The ratio declined somewhat in 1986-87, 1987-88 and 1988-89 to 2.0, 1.9 and 1.2 per cent respectively. Thus, in the first four years of the Seventh Plan (1985-86 -1988-89) the current deficit is estimated to have averaged at 1.9 per cent of GDP, as against 1.5 per cent during the Sixth Plan. These ratios underscore the current pressures on the balance of payments.

The balance of payments problems facing the country are likely to be acute in the years to come which calls for innovative approaches, appropriate corrective measures, and sustained and well-directed efforts for maintaining viability without constraining growth and capital formation in the economy.

Export Performance

The volume of exports has been steadily rising year after year except in 1965-66 and 1985-86. The combination of export promotion policies, especially since the mid 1980s and the buoyancy in world trade has began to have salutory effects on exports growth since 1986-87. Information on exports and their growth rates are presented in

Table-2. However, a glance at the data presented in Table-3 reveals that India's share of world trade is falling. From the 16th rank in the 1950s, it had declined to the 42nd rank in the 80s, her share falling from 2.1 per cent in 1950 to 0.4 in 1986.

Composition of Exports — Emerging Trends

Let us now examine the emerging trends in the composition of India's exports. Table-4 shows exports by major commodity groups during 1987-88, 1988-89 and the first half of 1988-89 and 1989-90.

Cashew exports showed a decline of 9.6 per cent during 1988-89 in value. The set back in export earnings from cashew arose from a fall in unit value realisation of 13.4 per cent, because of severe competition from other edible nuts. However, it is gratifying to note that export of cashew kernels during April-September, 1989 witnessed a substantial increase of as high as 35.9 per cent in value. Export earnings from tea in 1988-89 showed a marginal increase of 1.1 per cent in value and during the first six months of 1989-90 earnings from tea exports witnessed a substantial jump of as high as 36.7 per cent. So far as coffee is concerned there was a modest increase of 6.3 per cent in earnings despite a drop in export volume of 6.9 per cent during 1988-89. This was attributed to increase in unit value realisation of about 14.1 per cent. During April-September 1989 export of coffee showed a substantial increase of 43.4 per cent over that in the same period of 1988.[3] It is to be noted here that the international coffee market has been in a state of turmoil since July 1989 when the International Coffee Agreement (ICA) meeting decided to suspend the operation of the export quota system for two years from the first week of July 1988 instead of waiting until September, 1989 when ICA was due to expire.

Exports of marine products represented an increase of mere 20.4 per cent in value. During the first six months of

1989-90 export earnings from marine products showed only a marginal increase of 1.7 per cent. Japan is the major market for our marine products. With the expansion of acquaculture facilities for production of shrimp in Philippines, Thailand and Indonesia competition is expected to be intense. Japan is also the India's major destination for iron ore exports. Iron ore exports during 1988-89 was Rs. 672.5 crores which showed an increase of 16.2 per cent in volume and 23.9 per cent in value with a modest appreciation of 6.6 per cent in unit value over 1987-88. This trend has been maintained when earnings from iron ore exports increased by 34.8 per cent during the first half of 1989-90.

Leather and leather manufactures is a sector where India enjoys comparative advantage in terms of a large live-stock population and labour intensive character of the industry. The market for shoe uppers has been promising. The Indian leather and leather goods exporters bagged orders worth Rs. 60 crores during the "Semaine Du Cuir 1988", held at Paris from September 17 to 20. About 2073 exhibitors from various countries participated in the fair. India was represented by 65 exhibitors.[4] There has been stiff competition from China so far as footwear is concerned. Even though our shoes were better, there was resistance to their prices.

Export of spices which was valued at Rs. 250.8 crores in 1988-89 dropped by about 19 per cent in their value despite an increase in the volume by 12.9 per cent. This was again due to fall in unit value realisation by 28.3 per cent. In recent years exports of cardamom (small) have suffered for two important reasons, viz. higher prices in the domestic market and severe price competition in West Asia from Guatemala. In case of pepper which is the major item in the spices group, high standards of cleanliness required in our major markets have constrained exports. Exports of tobacco suffered a setback both in volume and value because of declining demand for tobacco in the world market due mainly to anti-smoking campaigns and government restrictions on consumption. Added to this, stagnant yeilds of tobacco in India, increased cost of cultivation and failure to produce quality tobacco are making Indian tobacco less competitive in the world market.

Export of engineering goods have shown a robust performance in recent years in spite of intensifying competition in the world market and erosion of import capacity of many developing countries which were India's important markets. In 1988-89 engineering goods witnessed an increase of 62.0 per cent. Exports of chemicals and allied products rose by 86.3 per cent during 1988-89 and by 30.6 per cent during the first half of 1989-90.

Exports of gems and jewellery spurted by 68.3 per cent in 1988-89. But this upward trend slackened to 37.1 per cent in the first half of 1989-90. This most dynamic non-traditional export sector faces problems such as increasing international competition, late recovery of export bills, etc.

Another non-traditional export item of no less importance is technical consultancy. Construction services and engineering design services form two important aspects of such an export item. World market for construction services is marked by overwhelming dominance of industrial countries who are able to offer attractive financial packages to fund such projects. Civil construction exports which were of the order of Rs. 168 crores in 1984 jumped to Rs. 178 crores in 1988 which is higher than the level of construction exports of Rs. 118 crores recorded in 1987.[5] The Exim Bank has been approaching various organisations and agencies to obtain more contracts in many developing countries. There has been a substantial increase in the technical consultancy contracts in 1987 and the technical consultancy contracts secured by the Bank in 1987 were of the value of Rs. 230 crores.

Even time has come to export components of two-wheelers from India. Honda Motors Ltd., the Japanese collaborator, one of the world's largest manufacturers of motor cycles, has evinced keen interest in buying components especially castings and forgings from its Indian partner Hero Honda Motors Ltd.[6] Opportunities should be exploited to increase foreign exchange earnings from this sector as well. There is scope for generating business worth US $100 million over the next five years from export of software. According to a delegation of Indian software companies to U.S.A. led by Mr. Saurabh Srivastava, Xerox Corporation, Visa International, Bank of America, Ask Computer Systems, Boeing Information Services and General Electric's information systems division have showed keen interest to buy software developed by Indian companies.[7] India may do well to concentrate on export of knowledge-intensive services. There are other services like data processing and type-setting by computer which are also potential candidates for service exports.

Direction of Exports : Emerging Trends

The destination-wise pattern of India's exports displays a clear diversification. In 1988-89, the share of exports going to industrial market economies as represented by OECD group was 58.2 per cent, while East Europe and developing countries accounted for a share of around 16.5 per cent each. The countries of the OPEC accounted for a market share of 6 per cent. Data presented in Table-5 reveal the trends on the direction of India's exports.

It is clear from the table that the bulk of exports from India to the OECD group went to the EEC, the U.S.A. and Japan. Exports to the EEC showed an increase of 25 per cent from Rs. 3,957 crores in 1987-88 to Rs. 4,946 crores in 1988-89. Exports to U.S.A. in 1988-89 rose by 28.5 per cent to Rs. 3,736 crores from Rs. 2,908 crores in 1987-88. Exports to OPEC group and East European countries showed an increase of 23.2 per cent and 29.4 per cent respectively. Exports to developing countries (excluding member countries of the OPEC) witnessed a substantial increase of more than 50 per cent.

The most important single economic event during the early nineties that is going to take place is the creation of a single European market. The twelve countries of Europe will emerge as an economic union and may build a fortress which the developing countries like India may find difficult to penetrate. It is here that a suitable export strategy for these countries requires to be worked out.

Jordan is also emerging as a potential market for Indian goods. Large Indian business houses are entering Jordan in a big way. Reliance Industries and Raunaq Enterprises have already committed themselves to set up two joint venture projects in Jordan at a total cost of $1.1 billion. The Birla Company CIMMCO is understood to have finalised a deal to put up a $40 million textile project in Jordan. Reliance has agreed to set up a 600,000 tonne phosphoric plant and Raunaq Enterprises a joint venture fertiliser project in that country.[8] These joint venture projects in Jordan would indirectly help boost export of plant and machinery from India in the sense that the Indian companies will contribute their share of investment through supply of plants and machinery.

Prospects for exports to Cyprus is encouraging. Addressing the members of the Federation of Indian Chambers of Commerce and Industry (FICCI) the President of Cyprus Mr. George Vassiliou said that Cyprus could be considered as gateway for exports to the European market.[9] He also urged the Indian businessmen to join hands with their Cypriot counterparts for setting up industrial ventures in that country not only for producing goods for the Cypriot market but for exports as well.

Thus the preceding review on balance of payment scenario, export performance, composition and direction of exports reveal the following major trends.

1. The BoP problems facing the country are likely to be

acute in the years to come unless well-directed efforts are made to boost exports on a substantial scale.

2. The volume of exports has been rising year after year and since 1986-87 the growth rate has been steadily improving.

3. There has been a shift in the composition of India's exports in favour of non-traditional items like gems and jewellery, consultancy services including construction and engineering design services.

4. Most of our products in the world market have been facing a severe competition particularly in terms of prices and quality.

5. There has been a high growth in exports to EEC, U.S.A. and Japan, and other developing countries of Asia (excluding members of OPEC). Jordan and Cyprus have also emerged as potential markets for our products.

6. India's exports may have to contend with uncertainty in East European market arising out of proposed economic reforms underway.

Export Promotion - The Government's Role

The government helps the exporters through various bodies such as Export Promotion Councils, Commodity Boards, Trade Representatives, etc. In order to increase exports we have so far relied on measures like export subsidies, duty-drawback scheme, export credit and credit insurance, the exchange risk administration scheme and currency depreciation.[10] Again with a view to giving impetus to export drive, government have set up Export Processing Zones (EPZs) which provide almost free trade environment for export production so as to make Indian export products competitive in the world market.[11]

Measures have also been taken for promoting exports of specific items. For promoting project exports in the non-traditional sector the government have provided a number of incentives which include market development assistance for reimbursement of 50 per cent of cost of preparation and submission of bids and project assistance to the extent of 10 per cent of net foreign exchange earnings from the service portion of the contracts. Powers have been delegated since May 1, 1989 to authorised dealers and the Exim Bank to grant pre-bid clearance for export of management / technical / consultancy services up to the monetary limit of Rs. 2 crores and Rs. 5 crores respectively. The Exim Bank has also set up a special group to enhance such exports.

With a view to improve the competitive position of Indian jute manufactures a number of incentives have been introduced. These include cash compensatory support for all exports of jute goods at an uniform rate of 12 per cent, additional incentive at the rate of 10 per cent over and above CCS adminissible on diversified jute products, and import of raw jute against export of jute goods under advance licensing scheme.

Further, interest rates on pre-shipment and post-shipment export credit were lowered by 2.0 percentage points and 0.85 percentage point per annum respectively. The rate of interest on pre-shipment credit up to 180 days was lowered from 9.5 per cent to 7.5 per cent. The same on pre-shipment credit beyond 180 days and up to 270 days was lowered to 9.5 per cent from the previous rate of 11.5 per cent. Interest rate on post-shipment credit for all categories of advances was reduced to 8.7 per cent from 9.5 per cent.

A brief mention may be made here about the new Exim Policy as enunciated by the National Front Government in March 1990. It is an export-oriented policy. Some of the important measures envisaged in the policy are :

1. The threshold limit for export recognition has been

reduced from Rs. 5 crores to Rs. 4 crores in net foreign exchange earnings.

2. To facilitate faster disposal of incentive applications, it has been decided to obtain affidavit from registered exporters on a quarterly basis with regard to realisation of export proceeds, instead of bank realisation certificate on monthly basis.

3. All processed minerals and ores, excluding iron ores, will now be entitled for export incentives. At the time of announcement of the Exim policy, minerals and ores were not entitled for export incentives.

Strategies — Some View Points

As has been seen earlier the rate of growth in export earnings in recent years has been somewhat impressive. But our share in the total world market has been less than one per cent till 1986. The Government have announced various promotional measures to boost exports with a view to bring down the BoP deficit to a manageable level. The projected data for exports during the nineties and the rate of their growth are given in Table-6. The rate of growth is likely to be around 12.7 per cent. Efforts to expand and diversify exports both by products and markets must continue for, 12.7 per cent growth cannot be considered as substantial. The Working Group on Exports under the Planning Commission has already projected the growth of 30 per cent per annum for sunrise products and 15 per cent for star products.[12] Sunrise products are those products for which global markets are growing fast, where India has an inherent comparative advantage and where current exports are small. Star products are those for which world markets are already large and India has a foot-hold. Thus, there is a difference of opinion in the rate of growth in exports. Anyway the growth per annum should be around 20 per cent and all-out efforts should be made to achieve this goal.

Recently the draft approach paper to the Eighth Plan has outlined a five-pronged strategy for export growth. This comprises the following:[13]

1. greater attention to expanding exports of labour-intensive manufactures which have emerged as dynamic elements in Indian trade,
2. strengthening of institutional infrastructure for exports such as export houses, export promotion councils and specialisation in both products and selected markets,
3. elimination of procedural bottlenecks,
4. rationalisation of incentives, speedy delivery of raw materials, equipment and components related to export production and promptness in provision of export assistance, and
5. emphasis on supportive exchange rates and demand management as well as adequate investment provision for infrastructure where there is a high concentration of export production industry.

The measures adopted so far have yielded some results but they are far too inadequate to meet India's needs and aspirations. Hence there is a need to change the strategy. If we want to penetrate global export market and increase our share in world's exports, the present policy of more "adjustments" in fiscal and financial incentives to exports should be replaced by a policy that would help setting up truly competitive production units. These production units should be in "thrust sectors" identified for exports. They should be assured of all inputs including machinery and technology. It may be pointed out that India's exports have suffered in terms of quality, price and marketing efforts. The technology gap has also created a hurdle resulting in cost disadvantage to Indian exports.

One of the areas that ought to attract the attention of

the newly industrialising countries including India is the manufacturing sector which is shrinking in the Western industrialised countries, in terms of its contribution to GNP. The U.S. and other industrialised countries will continue to need manufactured products which could be supplied by "new comers". What Korea, Taiwan and Mexico could do, India could also do, and perhaps better if the policy undergoes a change. Some of the measures to improve the performance of engineering exports sector include improvement in low productivity and quality of products, standardisation of components and maintaining delivery schedules. Consultancy exports have an important role in reducing the trade deficit of the country as each successful consultancy service would bring to the country an additional exports of at least ten times more than its original value, because of its multiplier effect. Hence, besides the incentives as prevailing at present to encourage this sector the suggestion of the Federation of Indian Export Organisations (FIEO) to give total income tax exemption for consultancy exporters could be considered by the government. The Exim Bank should also identify more and more project opportunities for the potential exporters.

Jewellery exports have yet to take off. Special efforts will have to be made to promote these exports. India will have to continue to concentrate more on low quality roughs which require higher labour input and in which we have comparative advantage. The demand for sports shoes has been rising all over the world. The Indian shoe industry needs to take up the challenge of meeting a part of this demand. Tourism has also proved its potentiality in contributing substantially to foreign exchange earnings. Hence it needs greater attention. India can also enter such fields viz., transistor radios, calculators, TV and the like vacated by some of the advanced industrial countries.

As has been mentioned already, there has been a high growth in exports to developing countries of Asia excluding of course, the members of the OPEC. Some of these economies like Korea, Singapore, Malaysia, Hong Kong and Taiwan have witnessed continued economic growth alongwith significant trade liberalisation and economic deregulation. These economies provide an excellent opportunity for export thrust.

The European markets which are sophisticated require different market strategies. We have to identify what they need rather than try to find markets for what we have. Effective and dynamic pricing policy constitutes an essential element of a dynamic marketing strategy, particularly with a view to achieving the desired rate of growth in exports. Less developed economies like ours suffer with a deficiency in respect of price competition mainly owing to their technological, managerial and financial constraints. Their efforts in this direction are thwarted by the technologically advanced and financially sound international competitors. A few cases may be cited here.

India suffers from price disadvantage with Japan in Thai Market. Similarly, it has been estimated that export marketing of Indian hand and cutting tools has been facing a price disadvantage of about 15 to 35 per cent; about 20 per cent in machine tools and between 30 to 50 per cent in tractors.[14] Thus, it may be inferred that technologically sophisticated products are *difficult to sell items* for developing countries like ours. However, despite all these limitations pricing strategy, if suitably devised is likely to lead to substitution of products coming from developed countries. Such a situation calls for selling below cost at least in the short run.

It is generally believed that low-priced goods coming from less developed countries are invariably of inferior quality. Hence, the old contention that low price leads to maximization of sales loses its weight in international marketing. However, effective publicity and demonstration are necessary which will add to the changing preference in favour of the low-priced goods. Of course, provided the importers are induced to import and distribute qualitative goods at low prices.

Conclusions

India will have to handle the export sector carefully as the global trade patterns are changing quickly. The economy has to be fairly flexible and responsive to signals, in order to enable it to reap the benefit from export-oriented strategy. A change in emphasis from traditional to non-traditional goods and from exports of goods in general to export of services wherever possible is called for. India will do better to adopt a selective approach to exports rather than dissipate energies on a large number of items. The Indian exporters should draw a lesson from the experiences of Japan, South Korea and Thailand which focussed on world market when they conceived and designed a product. They must bear in mind that quality, cost competitiveness and above all, marketing techniques are basic to capturing the world market. In other words, we have to identify what the market needs rather than try to find markets for what we have. Market analysis and study should prcccdc production schedules and patterns.

NOTES AND REFERENCES

1. *Economic Survey*, 1989-90, Government of India, p. 10.
2. Ibid.
3. Ibid, p. 120.
4. *The Indian Export Trade Journal*, Vol. XXXII, No. 10-11-12, Oct-Dec. 1988 (page not mentioned).
5. India's share in the world market for technical consultancy is hardly 1.5 million dollars.

   -Ibid.
6. *The Times of India*, June 13, 1990.

7. *The Times of India*, June 5, 1990.

8. *The Indian Export Trade Journal*, Vol. XXXIII, April-June, 1989, p. 14.

9. Ibid, p. 15.

10. Rupee depreciated against the Dollar, the Pound, the Yen and Deutche Mark by nearly 45, 22, 64, and 46 per cent respectively in 1988 compared to the base year 1990.

    -Trivedi, H.K. "Export Strategy for India in the Nineties" in Rajbahak, R.P. et al, *Export Strategies of '90s*, Anmol Publications, New Delhi, 1990, p. 5.

11. India has six EPZs located at Kandla, Santacruz, Falta, Noida, Cochin and Madras. The seventh EPZ at Vishakhapatnam was approved and notified on 15th March, 1989.

12. Trivedi, H.K. op. cit, p. 12.

13. *The Times of India*, May 25, 1990.

14. Roy, H. Lajipathi, "Indian's Foreign Trade : An Analysis", *Yojna*, Oct. 1-15, 1987, p. 24.

TABLE – 1

India's Balance of Payments : Key Indicators

(As per cent of GDP)

Year	*Exports*	*Imports*	*Trade Balance*	*Invisibles (Net)*	*Current Account Balance*
1950-51	7.1	7.1	(+) 0.0	0.5	(+) 0.5
1955-56	6.6	8.0	(-) 1.4	1.4	(+) 0.0
1960-61	4.5	7.7	(-) 3.2	(-) 0.3	(-) 3.5
1965-66	3.6	6.3	(-) 2.7	0.3	(-) 2.4
1970-71	3.8	4.7	(-) 0.9	0.4	(-) 0.5
1975-76	6.1	8.0	(-) 1.9	1.3	(-) 0.6
1980-81	4.8	9.2	(-) 4.4	2.8	(-) 1.6
1981-82	4.9	8.7	(-) 3.8	2.1	(-) 1.8
1982-83	5.1	8.4	(-) 3.3	1.7	(-) 1.5
1983-84	4.9	7.7	(-) 2.8	1.5	(-) 1.3
1984-85	5.2	8.1	(-) 2.9	1.4	(-) 1.5
1985-86	4.4	8.1	(-) 3.7	1.2	(-) 2.5
1986-87	4.5	7.7	(-) 3.2	1.2	(-) 2.0
1987-88	5.0	7.8	(-) 2.8	0.9	(-) 1.9
1988-89*	5.7	8.0	(-) 2.3	1.1	(-) 1.2

Source : Various Issues of Economic Survey, Government of India.

*Economic Times, April 20, 1989.

TABLE – 2

Trends in India's Exports

Year	*Exports** (Rs. Cr.)*	*Growth Rate (%)*
1950-51	606	24.9
1955-56	609	2.7
1960-61	642	0.3
1965-66	810	(-) 0.7
1970-71	1535	8.6
1975-76	4036	21.2
1980-81	6711	4.6
1981-82	7806	16.3
1982-83	8803	12.8
1983-84	9771	11.0
1984-85	11744	20.2
1985-86	10895	(-) 7.2
1986-87	12452	14.3
1987-88 (p)	15741	26.4
1988-89 (p)	20295	28.9
Apr-Dec 1989	---	38.3

* Including Re-exports. p = provisional

Source: DGCI&S, quoted in Economic Survey, 1989-90, Government of India, p. 118 & p. S-73.

TABLE-3

India's Share in World Exports

(Value in Million US Dollars)

Year	*World's Exports*	*India's Exports*	*India's Share (%)*
1950	n.a	n.a	2.1
1955	n.a	n.a	1.5
1960	n.a	n.a	1.2
1965	n.a	n.a	1.0
1970	313706	2026	0.6
1973	875500	4355	0.5
1980	1989867	8378	0.4
1985	1926536	8750	0.5
1986	2117343	9187	0.4

Sources: From 1950 to 1965, Rajbahak, R.P., et al., op. cit., p. 7. From 1970 to 1986 International Trade Statistics Year Book, United Nations, 1987, quoted in Economic Survey, 1989-90, pp. S-82 - S-83.

TABLE – 4

Exports by Selected Major Commodity Groups (Rs. Crores)

Sl.No.	*Commodity*	*1987-88*	*1988-89*	*% Change 1988-89 / 1987-88*	*Apr - Sept 1988-89*	*Apr - Sept 1989-90*	*% Change Apr-Sept 1989-90/1988-89*
1.	Cashew Kernels	306.7	277.2	(-) 9.6	154	209.3	35.9
2.	Coffee and Coffee Substitues	263.2	279.7	6.3	140.9	202.1	43.4
3.	Fish and Fish Preparations	525.1	632.5	20.4	290.6	295.5	1.7
4.	Rice	324.6	331.5	2.1	155.1	297.2	91.6
5.	Spices	309.3	250.8	(-) 18.9	155.7	145.0	(-) 6.9
6.	Tea and Mate	592.4	599.0	1.1	280.8	383.9	36.7
7.	Tobacco	134.6	128.5	(-) 4.5	76.2	85.2	11.8
8.	Iron Ores	542.8	672.5	23.9	282.7	381.1	34.8
9.	Engineering Goods (Machinery, transport equipments, metal manufacturing and iron and steel)	1433.0	2321.7	62.0	961.8	1323.2	37.6
10.	Chemicals and Allied Products (Basic Chemicals)	823.4	1534.0	86.3	687.5	898.1	30.6
11.	Jute Manufactures	242.8	249.9	2.9	110.2	124.8	13.2
12.	Leather and Leather Manufactures incl, garments and travel goods	1148.5	1489.5	29.7	695.6	833.3	19.8
13.	Readymade Garments	1792.1	2097.5	17.0	879.8	1309.8	48.9
14.	Handicrafts	3253.3	5194.2	59.7	2227.4	2993.0	34.4
	of which : Gems and Jewellery	2613.5	4399.0	68.3	1845.4	2530.1	37.1

Notes : 1. Figures on export of Oil Cakes, Raw Cotton, Sugar, Cotton Yarn/fabrics, Petroleum Products, etc., have not been exhibited.
2. Data provisional.

Source : Economic Survey, 1989-90, Government of India, p. 119.

TABLE – 5

Direction of Exports (Rs. Crores)

Sl.No. Country	1970-71	1980-81	1983-84	1984-85	1985-86	1986-87	1987-88	1988-89
1. OECD	769	3126	4367	5272	5532	7004	9256	11813
of which :								
EEC	282	1447	1756	2002	1929	2736	3957	4946
of which :								
a. France	18	147	157	191	203	271	375	432
b. FRG	32	385	375	488	513	733	1061	1237
c. U.K.	170	395	556	613	524	700	1033	1165
d. U.S.A	207	743	1396	1766	1974	2332	2908	3736
e. Japan	204	598	826	1029	1164	1334	1615	2162
2. OPEC	98	745	882	944	835	774	981	1209
3. Eastern Europe	323	1486	1610	2242	2294	2389	2593	3356
of which :								
a. G.D.R	25	49	64	80	95	88	106	183
b. U.S.S.R	210	1226	1306	1880	2006	1867	1971	2609
4. Developing Countries (excluding members of OPEC)	305	1286	1563	1441	1463	1871	2238	3361
5. Others	40	68	1349	1845	771	414	673	556

Source : Adapted from Economic Survey, 1989-90, Government of India, p. S-78

TABLE – 6

Projections of Exports and Growth Rate

Year	*Exports (Rs. Cr.)*	*Growth Rate* (%)*
1989-90	26000	--.-
1990-91	29300	12.7
1991-92	30000	2.4
1992-93	37200	24.0
1993-94	42000	11.4
1994-95	47200	12.4
1995-96	53200	13.1
1996-97	60000	12.9
1997-98	67700	12.8
1998-99	76300	12.7
1999-2000	86150	12.9

* Computed

Notes : a. Figures on exports for 1989-90 are estimates on the basis of trends with adjustments to correspond to the emerging trends.

b. Export projections have been made, assuming an average annual growth rate of 12.7 per cent for the period after 1989-90 at 1988-89 prices.

Source : Mehta, S.S., "India's Foreign Trade: Performance and Policy Options for `90s", Indian Export Trade Journal, Vol. XXXXIII, 7-8-9, Jul-Aug-Sep, 1989, p. 4.

8

The Strategic Export Marketing Mode for Small Scale Industries in India in 1990s

MOHAN L. AGRAWAL

A desire to succeed and the adoption of a strategic mode of marketing. These are the two generally found characteristics of the successful small scale exporters. Dr. Agrawal in his article here arrives at this conclusion by citing some examples and goes on to suggest the ways to achieve this strategic mode. He begins with the finding that the lacunae in the Indian exporters is not in their products but in their marketing. Those successful in exports are those with these characteristics or the off-shoots of large business houses. The upliftment of exports is in the hands of these small exporters, he continues, and their transition to the strategic mode has to be built around four pillars. Segmentation and positioning will make the beginning supported by packaging and branding. But, more importantly, the change in the attitude of the export marketers to consider the products as commodity and a better understanding of the cross-cultural consumer values will lead to success. In the end Dr. Agrawal cautions that export marketing is not meant for naives and novices, it requires a strategic orientation to succeed.

— EDITORS

EXPORT marketing is a very specialised area of marketing of any country whether belonging to the South or the North block of the globe. It calls for a different orientation and a unique set of marketing actions. These marketing efforts are shrouded in market unfamiliarity, customer resistance and regulations. Any attempt, therefore, to analyzing export opportunities and prescribing marketing strategies to small scale industries is almost akin to 'seeing through an opaque crystal ball'. The area is quite new and risky. For the start-ups small scale units themselves have an assortment of structural problems ranging from survival to government regulations. Further, these units have yet to develop an export culture. They are not adequately equipped to deal with the problems associated with export markets and have yet to emerge as 'marketers' as opposed to 'manufacturers of products'.

In a recent study (FICCI, 1989), it was reported that the most dominant problem of small scale units in India, is 'marketing' of products. Further, the need is felt that the small scale units must break free from 'production' or the 'product' orientation and adopt the 'marketing' orientation instead (Agrawal, 1989).

Thus, asking small scale industries to be 'export-led units' is indeed too much. Undoubtedly, there are cases where small scale units have made it big in exports. However, a majority of these successful units are the satellites of large business houses which have been set up to meet the export obligation of the promoter companies. The rest of them are simply 'commodity-oriented' exporters (Cotton, spices, tea, coffee, etc. are the 'darkest' examples of this genre). Only in handful of cases, the small scale units on their own have done well on the export front. Table – 1 provides some statistics in this regard.

TABLE – 1

The Export Status of Small Scale Industries

Particulars	*1984-85*	*1985-86*	*1986-87*
1. Total export share (%)	21.74	25.42	29.83
2. Value of export (Rs. in cr.)	2,553	2,769	3,648

These units when analysed for their success variables, depict a unique mode of marketing, the characteristics of which others might do well to analyse and emulate. In the following pages, therefore, I shall be highlighting four major pillars by illustrating the caselets of three successful small scale exporters.

The Three Caselets

(i). The Darjeeling Tea

Tea has traditionally been a major export from India, inviting the participation of both private and public business houses. Over the years, Darjeeling Tea has become synonymous to quality tea from India. Unfortunately, however, it became a generic name - like the Monopoly Game. Every exporter - even from neighbouring countries like Sri Lanka, used the term Darjeeling Tea with impunity for their tea. Tea Board of India has been the major sufferer of this as it led to a fall in quality and image of the real Darjeeling Tea. Price recovery was, therefore, a problem. Concerned over the fact, the Tea Board adopted a marketing approach for tea and supported it with adequate advertising efforts. Impressive results followed (Reported in the Advertising and Marketing, July 1989).

(ii). The Shehnaz Herbal Charm

Shahnaz, a female entrepreneur in Delhi, has emerged as one of the best known exporters of beauty aid products with herbal appeal to several countries. Adopting an innovative marketing mode, she created a niche for herself and set up a chain of franchise outlets in India. She became a household name for every Indian woman conscious of appearing better. The export earnings of Shahnaz are considerable. For this, the Institute of Marketing and Management, New Delhi, presented her with the award of 'Marketer of the year 1988', in the presence of the Vice-President of India.

(iii). XYZ Garments of Ludhiana

With the real name disguised for proprietory reasons, this small scale unit in Ludhiana is a leading exporters of ready-to-wear garments to several European countries. The unit first supplied garments like commodity but later perceived the trends in quality and fashion in export garments. It developed a wide range of casual and trendy garments for adults and kid-wear made from superior cotton. The export of these garments jumped to Rs. 18 crores in 1988 from Rs. 2 crores in 1984. It also created a sizeable surplus for the unit.

The above examples, seemingly unconnected, have two things in common : firstly, all had the desire to succeed in the export market and secondly, they adopted a strategic mode of marketing.

Strategic Mode of Marketing : The Four Pillars

(i). Breaking Free from the 'Commodity' Export

The first thing that these exporters had done was that they no longer exported 'commodity'. Instead they successfully converted commodities into 'products' by adding value to the customers. The commodities were upgraded by mixing tangible and intangible features of the products. Tea is a commodity, but adding a symbol of Darjeeling or the Tea Board of India was one of the many ways to create a product out of a commodity. These exporters kept in mind that products must offer a need-satisfying feature to its customers. Thus, 'benefits to the customers' was the key to this strategic mode of marketing. They were aware that while commodities are prone to the wildest price fluctuations and unstable market supply, products are not. Thus it makes a better economic sense in converting commodities into products and thereby concentrating on customer-needs rather than monitoring daily price fluctuation.

(ii) Adoption of the STP Marketing Formulae

Once the exporter identified the 'product' in a correct perspective, efforts were initiated to Segment, Target and Position (STP) the product/market. The market segmentation became necessary as the exporters realized that markets are basically heterogenous and have only clusters of homogenous buyers. Each cluster would respond in varying manner to the product and marketing efforts. For instance, even though the SAARC countries have a common heritage and are thereby homogenous, they are vastly different in their marketing responses. Hence, they must be treated as such.

The break up of a heterogenous market into homogenous segments call for targetting. It refers to analysing marketing alternatives and selecting the most suitable to serve keeping in mind the product offering. This selection is usually done considering the strengths and weaknesses of the exporters and includes considerations as accessability and subsantiality of the market segment.

The companies mentioned above decided to target some countries in the beginning even though their products could be sold elsewhere too. Market selection was thoughtful and premeditated.

The final component of the STP formuale is positioning. In export marketing, it refers to the process of installing exporters in the minds of the buyers and markets in desired slots *vis-a-vis* its competitors. This image and perception is built up on the key characteristics of the product and consumer benefits. Thus, 'purity' or the 'Real Darjeeling Tea' was the position for the Tea Board. 'Indian Cotton' was the image sought by the garment exporter and 'Beauty Through Herbs' was sought by Shahnaz.

(iii) Branding and Packaging

Only recently have the Indian exporters realised the charm and power of branding and packaging in persuading customers. Naturally, most exporters have been slow on this front.

Branding and packaging complement the effort in converting the commodities into products and approaching a market via the STP formulae. It quickly and effectively provides consumers with a summary evaluation of what they could expect the product to be. Branding promises a consistent product performance.

To these exporters too branding made a business sense. Not only their marketing effort yielded better results for their existing products, it also opened further opportunities for 'brand extension' and permitted other products to piggyride on the established brands. It effected economy in efforts and resources. Thus, the name Shahnaz was enough to sell a wide variety of cosmetic products. Tea Board's 'Darjeeling' trade mark was another example.

Packaging has emerged as a potent tool for the product to draw customers. To these exporters, packaging was no longer meant for containing and protecting the product through rough and tumble of physical transportation across the nations. Packaging served as promotool to these exporters instead. It conjured up an image that these exporters sought for their products. Thus, Darjeeling Tea was packed in a convenient foil packaging, the herbal cosmetics in their own distinctive style and the ready to wear garments in attractive packages. The packaging complied with not only the constraints that the market intermediaries had, it also met the various government regulations and customer preferences in the host countries.

(iv) Understanding the Cross Cultural Consumer Values

Although gaining a better understanding of the cross cultural consumption values is extremely important, it is easier said than done. Most countries respond with pronounced reservation and anxiety to any enquiry on their cultural value pertaining to their consumption styles. Further such studies are highly complex and time consuming. Higher funds requirement is another problem. However, certain basics that these exporters followed in this respect are given below.

a. They determined the underlying consumer values, their nature and the rate of change over passage of time. This was done by studying the type of products used in most countries to which their products could be a fit.

b. They appraised the matching of their products with the core and fringe values of consumption in the host countries. Thus Darjeeling Tea was intended to match the English style of consumption.

c. They determined the characteristics of shopping/ buying patterns of the host countries, and its fit with their products.

d. They designed appropriate promotion tools. The Tea Board, for instance, allocate Rs. 25 lakhs for its campaign of Darjeeling tea and about a quarter of this was paid to Saatchi and Saatchi Co. (UK). In the end, this investment paid off.

e. They determined appropriate distribution channels for their products. They realised that the culture of distribution in the host countries was far more cohesive and unique. All the above three companies attempted to analyse and profit from this analysis of the host countries.

What does all this add up to? It speaks about a strategic mode of marketing. Does it suggest that luck and time was favourable to these companies? It indeed does. It, nevertheless, clearly indicates that a few lessons an exporter must remember. These would, perhaps, make a difference between their success and failure. The small scale exporter would do well to remember and operationalise these variables if they wish to survive and grow. After all, the export markets aren't for naives and ignorants. Are they?

REFERENCES

1. Agrawal, M.L. (1987), "Marketing in the Ancillary Industries", *Indian Management*, December.
2. —— (1989), "Marketing of Health Food in Europe: Is the Experience Replicable in India?", *Management and Labour Studies*. July.
3. —— (1989), "Towards Creating a New Marketing Order (NEMO)", *Indian Business Environment* (Ed.).
4. Banner, W.H., (1978), *Successful Marketing*, Prentice Hall, Inc., Englewood Cliffs, New Jersey.
5. Kotler, P. (1977), "From Sales Obsession to Marketing Effectiveness", *Harvard Business Review*, Nov.-Dec., pp 66-75.
6. NCAER (1972), *Study of Small Scale Industrial Units*, New Delhi.
7. St. Thomas (1959), "A Basic Guide To Marketing for the Smaller Company", *Industrial Marketing.*, 44, July.
8. Vepa, R.K. (1984), *How to Succeed in Small Industry*, Vikas, New Delhi.

9

Marketing Research — A Key to Success

Some Emerging Trends

P. K. SINHA

Dr. Sinha in his paper has highlighted the present status of Marketing Research in India and the changes that are likely to take place in the years to come when it has to play its key role for marketing success. The author expresses concern over the lack of what is called **Research Culture** among the most Indian companies and wonders as to how MR is still confined to product only. However, time is changing and the Indian marketers cannot manage without studying the consumers before offering a product that will find a niche in their mind. The author further emphasises that traditional ways of segmenting and studying customers on demographic basis is making way for and profiling them psycholographically. More use of computers in the wake of information explosion is visualised. A shift is likely to take place from quantitative research and emphasis shall be put more in projective techniques like that of Consumer Fair. Dr. Sinha has suggested a number of strategic changes to overcome the prevailing misconceptions about Marketing Research and expresses his hope that research will be made an integral part of the total marketing system of any firm.

— *EDITORS*

IN 1911, Curtis Publishing Company, publisher of the Saturday Evening Post, formed the first commercial research "Unit". Research Department head Charles Coolidge Parlin made his mark by convincing Campbell Soup company executives to advertise in his publication.

Parlin collected garbage from Philadelphia's blue collar neighbourhoods and was able to prove that the post's working class readers were heavy users of canned soup. Campbell's managers had believed that only the wealthy could afford to buy the soap instead of making it from scratch. Parlin's research — unorthodox, but effective — convinced the soup company that the post reached the right audience.[1] This was the beginning of market research. Surely, an humble one. The growth wasn't rapid till World War II. Athough the first book on Marketing Research, had come out in 1920s, the real impetus was in the five years between 1978-83. Thirtynine per cent of the research departments of the companies came in this period. The majority are established in the recent 20 years period. It suggests that Marketing Research is still being established as a fixture of marketing effort. The outside agencies have also grown very rapidly since 1950. Today this business is estimated at $1.5 to $3 billion per year.[2] This is the US scene. In contrast the Indian market research is just out of its infancy. Today it is a 15 crore industry comprising of about 100 firms. The expenditure on marketing research is very low. It ranges from 1 per cent to 1.3 per cent of sales with 2/3 of them spending less that 0.04% per cent of their sales.[3]

This trend is due to one basic reason: Absence of *Research Culture* among most of the companies. There is a lack of planning and effort on the part of research managers and agencies. Research is not considered to be an ongoing activity. Therefore, most of the companies do not have their own research departments. Research is taken totally on an ad hoc basis (70 per cent).[4] It is like, the manager thought that we should research and it is done. It is based more on the fancy of the manager rather than the need of the organisation. The area of research is also decided on the influence a manager has on the top management. Sometimes, the waiting line principle is applied. In a year everybody should get a chance to conduct research in the area of his/her interest. The top management's whims and fancies also determine the area of research. The "in-things" are considered for research.

The use of research is also restricted to the more tangible things, such as product. Channel decision got the least priority and the new product decision the most.[5]

The research is also misused, sometimes to support one's viewpoint and sometimes to grab power and authority. But the main problems are that it is considered superficial and in unauthentic and used only as a data collection technique. Analysis and interpretation are most primary or absent and hence the ideas come in numbers. There is also a lack of meaningful dialogue between marketing management and the research team. This is because the approach towards Marketing Research is not wholistic. There is also no specific budget allocated for research in most of the companies. The market research is mostly resorted to while making an investment decision. That too, primarily, to satisfy the financial institutions. This tendency is there because of the mental status that a 'licence to produce' is the 'licence to make money'. They are too sure to succeed.

The Future

Change in the Consumer Profile

It was a scene of 1980s where business succeeded because of technology. Any offer with a Japanese tag was a passport to success. Customers were enticed by features of the products which were used to differentiate among products. The liberalization of import policies brought world famous brands to India for the first time and it was received with open arms.

But these also brought along a boom in communication and the process was so fast that within no time there was information overload. Instead of helping the consumers decide, the messages started confusing them. In the process, however, the consumers got wise and knowledgeable about its needs, wants, desires, rights, and power. Now the customer cannot be towed away. The only option left to marketers now is to study the consumers and offer product that will find a niche in their mind than the market place. This is achieved through consumer analyses. The traditional ways of segmenting and studying customers on demographic basis is making way for profiling the customers psychographically and based on Values and Life Style (VALS).

Examples are being provided by shoes, readymade garments, etc. Even the tendency to consider each customer as a separate segment is on the rise. This will bring *Maxi-Marketing* to the forefront. It will require creating a large database for individual customers. In such situations Marketing Research is a key tool for success.

Geographic Scope Expansion

Two areas which were till now neglected will be attended to in the coming years. A vast rural areas and a highly competitive export market. The rural area has been supposed to be primitive and expected to have no takers of the products manufactured in the urban areas. But the expanded media coverage, mainly through television, has brought a change in the buying patterns of the rural mass, emerging as a big market for urban products led by consumables like soaps and edible oil and durables like TVs and vehicles. A marketer can no more ignore this area of development. Hindustan Lever has proved it time and again. The two market segments, urban and rural, are significantly different and hence the findings of one cannot be utilised to formulated products and strategies for the other. Larger part of the villages is illiterate and thus the quantitative research asking for ranks and ratings may not prove as effective as the qualitative research. The lead is provided by consumer fairs, pionered by XLRI, Jamshedpur and modified to suit the rural masses by XIM, Bhubaneswar.

World market has been highly competitive. India has been featuring in it mainly due to its traditional goods where it has a comparative advantage. The recent trends, however, show a growing portions of non-traditional exports, like technical consultancies to less developed countries and software to USA. These and some turn-arounds in traditional goods, like Darjeeling Tea, have been possible only because of a shift to a marketing orientation of the marketers. The essence of this lies in designing strategies based on the information from the importing countries and understanding the cross-cultural values. The expanding export market of non-traditional goods is the expansion of the marketing research activities to the export front, a sure sign of progress in the right direction.

Ripenning of Quantitative Research

Marketing Research will surely come into its own. The urge to succeed and the need to make correct and timely decision will require a very efficient Marketing Research System. The computers will no longer be confined to accountants and engineers. Marketing managers will have to depend on it in the wake of information explosion. It will be required more to use advanced statistical techniques that could not be performed manually and give more detailed analysis of information. The decisions are to be supported by hard facts to remove the subjectivity. Methods like Factor and Conjoint Analysis will be used for product designs. Positioning will require Multi Dimensional Scaling to be used extensively as the market will be full of brands, each brand indicating a product instead of the converse, and finding a portion will not be an easy task. Segmentation on Psychographic/VALS will require Cluster Analysis.

It is not just the consumers that will be the source of information. Even the channels must have to be managed most contemporarily. Efforts to be different will be in the lines of Marketing Channels also. A better dealer relations, a necessity, will require knowing the dealers better. This is possible only with a continuous dialogue with them requiring continuous flow of information and its analysis.

The situation of market will force the companies to diversify or look for other segments for their growth. In a competitive market this is also a tactical decision requiring full information and quick decisions.

Coming of Qualitative Research

The development on the quantitative front will also bring the Qualitative Research (QR) into vogue. This will put emphasis on focus group, in-depth interviews and other projective techniques.

Qualitative Research tries to look deeper into the behaviour of the consumer, beyond the expressions by hard data. It tries to find out as to why did people behave in a particular manner and what message did they arrive at out of the marketing exercise. For example, the answer to the question, "Did you like the advertisement?" would be a problem. "Yes, I did like it". This is said to please the questioner. The important thing to be found out is whether he identified with the advertisement; "Did he relate to it?", "Did he emote with the advertisement?", Did he feel, "this is my kind of brand", Did he feel, "My god, what have I been doing all these years? I haven't used the brand. May be I should.[6] In short, QR tries to read between the lines the latent and sublimal attitude of the respondent. It helps him to express more than what he wishes to express without realizing it.

However, the QR has to remove some of the misconceptions[7] before it can be accepted totally. The very first doubt coming up in the mind is : Opposed to the quantitative research, isn't QR subjective as it is dependent on the dialogue between the researcher and the respondent? Secondly, Is QR valid and reliable when a small sample is assumed to be representative of a large population? Thirdly, the respondent may say one thing during the group discussion, he may do the other. Finally, it is very much possible that the responses may be decoded differently by different research leading nowhere. These misconceptions will get cleared as one uses more of QR, since the quantitative research fails to show the expressions. It judges only on the basis of the rationalization of inquiries. Moreover, these views crop up because QR is seen through the eyes of a quantitative researcher and it is expected to fulfill the specifications of quantitative research.

The major QR methods involve Group Discussions and In-depth Interviews. In both the cases Projective Techniques are extensively used. Some of these techniques are shown in Annexure – 1. All these techniques try to bring out the inherent feelings of the respondents.

Suggested Strategic Changes

The nineties will see these misconceptions being overcome. In order that this is achieved some strategic changes will have to be brought. Firstly, the research will have to be made an integral part of the marketing organization. It has to contribute effectively to be acceptable and without any place granted to research it will not be taken seriously. It has also to be made clear that this will be a staff function supporting the line marketing executives. This has to be the responsibility of the top management. Unless there is total support from it, the total acceptance is impossible. A spirit of interactions and trust has to be developed between the researcher and the user: An unseen bond which creates *made-for-each-other* situations. Secondly, the misunderstanding of the use of research has to be removed. The research is to aid decision making and therefore, has to precede it. It does not have to be used for proving the authenticity of the decision. Also, the lack of knowledge about the use of research has to be removed. The scope and applicability of research is a debatable question in the sense that should the use of research be limited to only products or other areas should also be covered, for instance, distribution and consumer behaviour. The third corrective step is to clarify on the cost-benefit analysis of the research. Since the benefit out of research is non-monetary, namely a help in decision making, it is only the cost that is seen. The cost of wrong decision is mostly overlooked. The misconception about costlines of the research has to be removed by showing the benefits of correct information against the cost of imperfect information, both being reflected in the profit/loss due to a decision. The costs of research can also be reduced by widening the scope of research to include related areas at a marginal cost than conducting separate research for individual area. Further, the decision to deal with the present problem posed mostly by competition, invites decisions like price cuts, extra commission, etc. The urgency of decisions does not allow the research to be undertaken systematically. This will be taken care of by conducting research continuously rather than sporadically. This is possible only where the research is conducted on a planned basis and is considered to be a part of the decision making process and not simply a data collection exercise. It also generates a wrong notion that research is the fancy of only large organisations. This has to be corrected. This situation arises when the company is either short-sighted in its objectives or facing an intense competition. In the latter case, the urgency of decision does not allow the research to be conducted. In the former case, since the company does not take a tactical decision it doesn't see the need to know the consumer. It generally conducts "quick and dirty" research. In any case, the lack of information on part of the manager is responsible for such a situation and not the research. Research does not have any in-built mechanism to help a large organization or a smaller one. However, a company with a deep purse is benefitted to the extent that it can carry on the research for a longer period and in more varied areas. Consequently, the extent of use of research is related to the size of the firm but, it has no relation with the number of products/services offered. It is also found that above average firms spend more and are more likely to go for research.

Conclusion

The research in marketing is coming in its own, forced by the dynamicity of consumers and the intensity of competition. However, Indian firms are yet not using it to the fullest. The main reason for this is the absense of 'Research Culture' in the organisations. Research is not considered to be an integral part of the organisations.

But the 1990s will require the organization to wake up and start working in the directions of developing the culture of research. The time to come is going to see innovation strategy moving away from technology and key will be in knowing your customers better and trying to keep ahead of competitors through information. This will make research the centre of activities requiring several quantitative and qualitative techniques. However, few misconceptions have to be removed from the minds of the users and the researchers before it can be put to the maximum use.

REFERENCES

1. 'Garbage Dump Marks Long Beginning of Market Research', *Advertising Age*, Apr. 20, 1980, p. 68.
2. Peter D. Bennet, *Marketing,*, McGraw Hill, 1988, p. 153.
3. 'Strategic Failures', *Business World,* June 22-July 5, 1988.
4. 'Why MR Is Ineffective', *Business World,* Aug. 5-18, 1989, p. 19.

5. *Business India*, November 17-30, 1986.

6. Meena Kaushik, 'The Use of Qualitative Research in Developing and Testing Advertisement', Proceedings of Advertisement Seminar, *Deccan Herald*, Bangalore, 1987, p. 23.

7. Basker S. Ayer, 'The Coming of Qualitative Research', *Business World*, Nov. 8-21, 1989. pp. 13-15.

ANNEXURE — 1

Some Projective Techniques

A projective technique is a method by which people can express themselves freely by externalising their beliefs, their attitudes and their experiences in some symbolic or narrative form. This technique assumes that consumer behaviour is not always rational. When we present ourselves to the world we are not in any way eager to present the real self. We present ourselves with all our masks on and even when we are viewing an advertisement, we have got our masks on. Some of the techniques to look beyond the masks are given below.

a. Completion Techniques

These techniques are used in a group situation where you do not want any kind of group bias. You don't want views which are influenced by other respondents in the group.

Completion techniques are also very gainfully used and are important when we want to transfer the respondent's attitudes. When you know that he has very hardened attitudes and he does not want to verbalise them, then you can use the completion technique.

b. Cartoon Completion

This is one way of eliciting how people feel about any product or issue. This picturisation is what we call cartoon completion.

c. Association Technique

You take a stimulus word and ask for a free association. For instance when you show an advertisement to a respondent and you ask him what come to his mind, he says 'freshness', you then ask him what else comes to his mind and he says 'green' and you build on it to identify those elements of advertising which are salient and evocative of the right message.

d. Relationships

This is a very useful technique which through a brand marriage helps elicit those attributes of a brand that work best at motivating purchase. It also identifies the need(s) that this brand leaves unfulfilled *vis-a-vis* other brands.

e. Personification Techniques

This technique is used where you give brand human characteristics. You ask consumers to personify the brand. You tell them to give it a human look, human characteristics, a human figure. On the whole you ask them how do they personify a particular brand.

f. The Nightmare Technique

It is a very interesting technique in getting to the subliminal biases that one might have, but is not willing to verbalise. This technique is very often used when we are doing new product research and advertising research.

g. Projected Pictures

These are used very often in creative research when we are developing advertising, when we want to find out what kind of users we want to project in the advertising.

h. Psychodrama

Psychodrama is a technique used when we want to find out how people are reacting to a particular product, a particular brand. This is very useful when you are developing advertising. i.e. creative development for an advertisement.

i. Obituary Technique

It is used to elicit brand or corporate image. This basically gauges the relationship between the consumer and his brand and the loyalty which it engenders and the extent to which it could be replaced by another. The objective of this exercise is to determine the extent of brand loyalty by finding out how irreplaceable the brand is to the consumer.

j. Marketing / Fair

To create the mood, the researcher tries to put the respondent at ease or at a desirable frame of mind by asking a few general questions before the specific questions. It is, in fact, an exercise in developing rapport. This is where Marketing Fair comes in. The Marketing Fair as the name implies, is just that; a fair with all arrangements for fun and frolic with a slight difference. The set up of a Marketing Fair is just the same as a fun-fair, but in the former case the stalls have games designed to produce desired results. Regular games, like Hoopla, Darts, Card Games, 'Guess the Weight' etc. are also played. But each game is built around gathering data from the Players or respondent. As a result, the respondent approaches the game in a spirit of fun and as he is more concerned about winning the game and winning the prize, he is more likely to give subconscious but honest answers.

The fair of the type being discussed here is an application of the projective techniques of interviewing which allows respondents to project or express their own feelings as characteristics of someone or something else. It is a novel tool for data collection from the consumers. It is the only technique where the sponsoring/client companies can physically observe the actual data collection process, as it progresses. The fair aims at bringing together the consumer and business houses, to fine-tune products to actual customer expectations, with improved profitability to companies as well.

10

Profile of the Indian Consumer and the Role of Mass Communication

J.S. GIRI RAO

&

D. PANIGRAHY

Prof. Giri Rao and Prof. Panigrahy in their paper have highlighted some of the relevant aspects of the profile of the Indian consumer, his life style and buying behavior. The changing life style of the Indian consumer both in rural as well as urban areas has a tremendous impact on the marketing planning and control. The authors have discussed about the group motivation and opinion leaders. Some of the challenges to be witnessed in the Indian market during the 90s have also be examined. Towards the end Prof. Giri Rao and Prof. Panigrahy have given a brief idea of the scenario of mass communication and its role.

— *EDITORS*

OURS is a country of villages. Nearly 76 per cent of the population lives in rural India. The average membership of a household in rural India is 6.7 persons as against 5.8 per household in urban areas. The population is dominated by SC and ST population. The per capita income is low. So also literacy. With this an attempt is made in this paper to present a profile of the Indian consumer, his buying behaviour, the challenges for 90s to the marketers and the role of mass communication.

Profile of the Indian Consumer

The profile of the Indian consumer can be discussed in terms of literacy, sex ratio, income, urban-rural character, age-group, etc.

Age

About 80 per cent of the Indian population is below 40 years. Of which 42 per cent is below 14 years that are only consumers and not buyers. 5 per cent of the population is above 65 years and on the whole 75 per cent of the population has been born after 1950. The life expectancy has risen from 50 years in 1947 to 64.7 years in 1982.

Sex Ratio and Literacy

The male population of India is 52 per cent and the female population is the rest 48 per cent. Male literacy is 36.16 per cent i.e. approximately one out of every two males is literate. Female literacy has almost doubled in the last 20 years and now nearly one out of every four females is literate. The gap in male and female literacy is gradually narrowing.

In Kerala, Chandigarh and Delhi, the literacy rates are as high as 63-70 per cent with very little difference in male and female literacy. On the other hand, Uttar Pradesh, Madhya Pradesh, Bihar, Andhra Pradesh and Rajasthan — the largest States in India — are far behind in literacy. The male literacy in these States varies between 25 and 31 per cent and the female literacy between 15 and 22.

Rural-Urban Character

Nearly 76 per cent of the India's population lives in rural areas. Out of the total urban population, 50 million people live in only 20 towns and cities.

Income

48 per cent of our population i.e. about 335 million

people live below the poverty line which makes approximately six crore families. Out of this, population that live above the poverty line 54 per cent live in urban areas and 46 per cent in rural areas. The population living below poverty line i.e. 335 million both in urban and rural areas have no disposable income and hence no purchasing power. 18 crores of rural population have purchasing power but only a small portion of them can be reached through mass madia, less than half of them are literate. 195 million people in the urban areas who are above poverty line, can be reached through mass media. At current prices, the per capita income in 1981 was Rs. 1919 as against Rs. 466 in 1951.

The conclusions that we can draw from the preceding review is that approximately 100 million adults in the rural areas are the target consumers. Almost all marketing efforts and advertising in India are aimed at this section of the population.

Consumer Life Style

The joint family system has been broken down almost completely in the urban areas giving rise to nuclear families. The breaking down of joint family system has also started in the rural areas. One finds that the urban population spend more and saves less. They spend on education, entertainment, consumer goods, etc. The case of rural population is just the reverse. Eating and living habits of people in urban areas are changing. They spend more on time saving gadgets, health, foods, cloth, etc. The rural rich are fast catching up with their urban counterparts.

Buying Behaviour

Understanding the buying behaviour of the consumer is the pivotal factor for mass communication in the field of marketing as an essential part of advertising. An American concept being that *An advertising agency should be an extended home* clearly indicates the importance of consumer behaviour as a part of group behaviour, their values, their aspirations, the motivating factors applicable to them and lastly, the opinion leaders of the group under consideration. The trade secret and expertise is in understanding the psychology of the recipient group and serving the message in such a manner that the target audience accepts it with not much difficulty. As we are selling a product or service on somebody's behalf and our main purpose is of motivation, the concept of Group Psychology becomes extremely important than even in an individual, bilateral relationship motivations required to make the other person to be with you, for your thinking processes and perceptions to be at par. Similarly, in advertising, the Ad man has to know how the consumers will accept the product or service. He has to have the *gut feel* to know exactly the needs and levels of perception of his target audience. The values and perceptions for the Advertiser himself have to be overruled and he has to have an objective involvement. The product should offer such services which bring about ego fulfilment for the consumer and appeal to his identity.

Group Motivation

Group motivation can be brought about by, first attacking the opinion leaders. We are basically from rural and agricultural communities with established social hierarchy with the village elders, priests, school teachers, sarpanch, etc. as opinion leaders. Their certificate and testimonial are important to motivate the rest of the group which looks up to them. But in cities, towns, etc., the opinion leaders are not so obvious; at times they may have to be created to make the motivational strategies successful. In this case, a sample could be selected and preliminary research carried out by personal contact and get to know their requirements, values, connections, aspirations, means, etc. Then from that very sample, select your opinion leaders and present their personal experiences, through a persistent personal campaign, to the others in the group to motivate them into action. This kind of reference will have a tremendous amount of credibility and will act as a strong testimonial. So, first we find out the opinion leaders who can influence the group at a personal level e.g. a reputed and known doctor in a colony. Opinion leaders need not be people from higher strata but one of the very group selected. It is very important to know that for every product or service there will be a different group with a different set of opinion leaders.

Challenges of 90s

Growing awareness among the consumers and rising prices of goods and services have created in consumers an attitude to expect best quality. Consumers have become very cautious and choosy and conscious of their spending because of existing inflation factor in our country.

The companies dealing with household appliances made a point to have customer service cells. This trend of setting up customer service cells, has also encroached even in firms dealing with/manufacturing cosmetics, toiletries, etc. Many companies started holding service weeks in various parts of the country where appliances regardless of age or type of defect, are repaired free of charge. Many producers/manufacturers of goods solicit complaints from the consumers by providing inland letters for speedy flow of information.

The increase in literacy rate and hike in the incomes of the people has also encouraged the consumers to accept the consumer movement as the need of the day. The old and recent legislation intended to save and protect the consumer's interest in the country have generated an understanding for the product awareness among the consumers about their rights and remedies and safeguards available to them.

Besides growing consumerism, the purchasing power

of the consumer is likely to shrink except in the hands of narrow elite - rural and urban - because of inflation and transfer of resources from poor to rich. The boosting of elite market both urban and rural will be constantly on the increase stressing more qualitative than quantitative expansion. General demand for quality product at reasonable price will be more wilder than the present market conditions.

The product competition will be so intense that in turn, it would create increasing industrial sickness of medium and small units. Stagnation of markets are predicted and stricter control over marketing budgets will be imposed, with fierce competition for greater share of narrow market.

Greater pressure on advertising to create consumer ideology and to invent new products is foreseeable. In addition manipulative advertising is likely to be encouraged. Here the government can play a big role by enacting suitable legislation and also the court of law by upholding the principle "let the seller beware" by taking into account the interest of the consumer in modern marketing situation.

Role of Mass Communication

It is an admitted fact that high degree of illiteracy exists in rural India, with exception to certain areas in the South and in Bengal. Problems relating to media arise due to poor readership in the villages. At the district level readership is pretty good. Advertisements in local magazines and newspapers have good readability, with village elders/intellectuals. There are less than 15 newspapers for every 1000 people. 50 per cent of the total circulation of newspapers is confined to the four metropolitan cities and hardly 2 per cent of the copies circulate in rural India. The literacy rate has to be increased to understand and accept the product information for product consumption usages. In order to achieve this, the industry has to take initiative in adopting the villages for adult education and sponsoring newspaper for subscription in which their products are advertised.

Radio, the most popular and cheapest medium, which has covered 90 per cent of Indian territory geographically and 85 per cent of population demographically, is an important tool in communicating the message across. Product information, product education and services could be transmitted for target audience utilising the services of local talents, languages, dialects and usages. Folk dramas and songs are best suited for developing product image and industry's credibility. There are 40 million radio receivers in India out of which 20 million sets are in rural areas.

Out of the total 10,000 cinema halls in India, 8,000 are in the urban areas. The four South Indian States and Maharashtra have nearly 60 per cent of the total theatres. The elitist color with Western ideology prevailing in the industry's advertisements should be made as the thing of the past. Industry must learn to understand the importance and relevance of rural targets.

With the advent of satellite communication, the rise in television communication is manifold since 1984. There are, presently in India, 530 television relay transmitters situated through out the length and breadth of the country and communicating messages approximately to 85 per cent population of various languages/dialects. This is the only audio-visual medium which has got the spontaneous impact on target audience. The industry and manufacturers should realise and understand the importance and coverage of this medium and come forward to donate community television sets (preferably colour televisions) to villages for tapping and motivating the targets for product mobilisation. It is not enough to brush their shirts after installing the television sets at villages. They also should provide timely post-installation services for television sets and depute, block-wise, sales personnel equipped with a VCR for introduction of their product or the new information about the product. It has to be kept in mind that for every programme made in terms of video by the industry, the local talents, i.e., the sarpanch, the school teacher, village workers, the doctor, respectable elders, etc. are to be involved in order to gain and develop the belongingness among the rural folk. It, in other words, will develop the credibility of the industry and gain the acceptance of the product.

In the light of circumstances, we can conclude that, mass communication would play a pivotal role in developing consumerism in India by creating more awareness among the consumers and by making them better informed. By the time we enter 21st century, mass communication would become indispensable to raise the standard of living and change the life styles, and it would gain equal importance from both the sellers and the buyers.

REFERENCES

1. *The Economic Times*, December 5, 1982.
2. *The Times of India*, May 27 & 31, 1990.
3. *India 1988*, Government of India, New Delhi.
4. *Televisions in India*, Directorate General of Doordarshan, New Delhi, 1988.
5. *Census*, 1981.
6. *Report of Registrar of News Papers of India*, 1988, New Delhi.

11

Emerging Trends in Promotion

S. GOVINDRAJAN

Eighties was a watershed decade and Nineties is going to be the decade of the fruition of the efforts put in 80s, Prof. Govindrajan in this article points out that the beginnings made in the areas of positioning, comparative ads, political ads and the shelf space acquiring will reach their pinnacle in this decade. He also maintains that rural markets will gain importance and Direct Marketing will begin to gain prominance. There is no Average Indian Consumer and thus the segmentation by demographic variables has become redundant. Comparative advertising is going to be an established phenomenon. The human mind being the slate, the darkest chalk will be most visible and hence positioning will be the key to success. Television, he feels, that was the tool to success in 80s is now just another media. This will lead to use of other innovative media and direct marketing is what marketers are looking forward to. Prof. Govindrajan ends with a remark that in such a context the years to come promise to be an exciting future for the Marketing Men.

— *EDITORS*

THE Eighties has been regarded by many as a watershed decade for Indian Marketing. This decade saw the beginning of the *Positioning Era*, Comparative Advertising, Political Advertising, the growing importance of Shelf Space at retail outlets, the importance of rural markets and the beginnings of the conception of *Direct Marketing* as a philosophy. All these were governed by a common denominator : a quantum increase in competition. The Nineties should see the crystallisation of many of these changes and the beginnings of some new trends as well.

"Watsonian Behaviorism", propounded by psychologist John Watson as far back as the 1930s likens the human being's mind to a blank slate at birth. The most impressions on this slate are made by those who use the darkest chalk to write on it. This is what positioning is all about. Needless to say, the greater the competition, the greater the importance of positioning. Let us go back to the analogy of the chalk and the slate. The greater the number of brands in the market place, the greater the number of chalks with which to make impressions on the human mind. Thus, the the need to have an impression which cannot be erased becomes crucial in order to remain in the consumer's mind. As can be seen in the Indian context, sharply defined positions such as those of "Lifebuoy", "Onida", "Godrej Storwel", etc. were the brands to enjoy high brand share. What gives the concept of positioning greater credibility is the established linkage between Brand Share and "Top of the Mind Recall". Thus, the next decade will see a scramble by marketers to get brands to the top of the consumers' minds. To try and get picked off the shelves first.

Comparative advertising is the natural manifestation of a highly competitive environment. While it has become *de rigueur* in USA, it is comparatively a new phenomenon in India. The first real comparative advertisement in India was released more than a decade ago by Nutramul when it compared prices of competing brands. That, however, was an isolated case. Today, the cases of HCL Copiers vs Modi Xerox, TVS Suzuki vs Hero Honda, Nirma vs Surf Nirma vs Rin and BPL vs Videocon are clear indications that comparative advertising is here to stay. A lot is being said about this phenomenon and the debate as to whether this is ethical or not is a hot one. This was exactly what happened in USA about a decade or so ago. The debate has long since subsided there and Comparative Advertising is an established phenonmenon. In India, this is likely to happen in this decade. The reasons are not hard to find. Going back to the chalk and slate analogy, the only way a newcomer or competitor can make an impression in the human mind is to erase the earlier impression and this may entail a comparison.

Can a political party or its candidate be sold as a product is? Yes, if the British and American examples are anything to go by. The much publicised campaign of Saatchi and Saatchi for the Tory Government of Margaret Thatcher and the usage of advanced lab techniques in George Bush's campaign have ensured that Advertising is an integral part of the campaigning procedure in these countries. In India, too, a start has been made in this regard. The 1984 elections saw the Congress-I using Rediffusion's services to develop an Advertising campaign. The 1989 elections had the Congress repeating this. The newest addition was the concept of "Video on Wheels", used by Devi Lal, much on the lines of the "Chaitanya Ratham" of N.T. Ramarao. Hence, the Eighties were the "experimental" phase insofar as Political Advertising was concerned. The Nineties should see this becoming part and parcel of election campaigns.

A lot has been said about "Consumer Pull", or the ability of the brand to have consumers demand the product at the retail outlet. The heady days of a large number of brands enjoying this quality has become history. Today, the number of such brands is low and rapidly diminishing in number. How else can one account for the success of "Gold Cafe" against the might of "Nescafe"? The naked truth of the market place is : To sell a product it has to get into the retailer's shelf in the first place. And getting the product into the shelf and having the retailer push it has become a gargantuan task. Thus one of the most important objectives of any Marketing Manager in the last decade was: Procuring a spot on the retailer's shelf so that the consumer can see it easily and getting the retailer to push it just in case the consumer does not spot it. Thus, incentives and margins for retailers and dealers became an important variable to be tackled. Thus dealer display contests, aggressive merchandising and efficient retailing have become the fulcrum around which Marketing Plans revolve. This is going to be more hectic in the 90s.

Ironically, the variable which helped bring about strong consumer pull in the early eightics has been instrumental in doing away with it. Television, which burst into prominence during the 1982 Asiad helped a number of brands gain a truly national identity. The most spectacular example was Nirma. Television as a medium offered tremendous reach coupled with the standard advantage of any Audio-visual medium. It had audio as well as video to help you drill messages into the consumer's mind. Coupled with the middle class boom, this medium helped a number of brands rocket to the top. The problems surfaced later. Today, clutter has become a big problem for advertisers. It is a Catch-22 situation. If you schedule the spot with a programme with a poor rating, nobody watches it. If you schedule it with a programme with a high rating, there are so many advertisements that you are not sure that your advertisement has been noticed. When you consider the fact that a program like Mahabharat has as many as 33 spots scheduled before it, you realise the enormity of the problem. Thus the human mind has become an inadequate container to store the names of all these brands. This has brought about three changes. First, the consumer pull which some brands enjoyed in the early eighties has been considerably diluted. Secondly, a new marketing term has entered the lexicon - "Salience" or the ability of the advertisement to be noticed and remembered. Consequently, to gain salience the quality of television advertisements have shown a dramatic improvement. Thirdly, advertisers no longer blindly pump in major portions of their advertising budget into television. Budget outlays in other media and Sales Promotion in particular have shown increases. The other spin-off has been the emergence of the Philosophy of

Direct Marketing.

What is the "Average Indian Consumer"? The truth is that there is no average Indian Consumer. How else can one explain the fact that Mustard Oil, which is a fast moving item in Coastal Orissa, has sluggish movement in Western Orissa? Why is it that "Capstan" outsells "Cavenders" in many districts of Orissa while being outclassed in some other districts? Thus, the concept of the "Average Indian Consumer" is just a statistical concept. Hence, the days of segmentation on broad demographic variables like age, sex, etc. are gone. The days of "Direct Marketing" are here. "Direct Marketing" to most people signifies traditional mail order catalogues. While it is true that this constitutes a major portion of Direct Marketing as it exists today, the term itself is used to denote a way of thinking. Direct marketing is a process by which a marketer attempts to build up a loyal consumer franchise by catering to the individual needs of each consumer. Sounds fantastic? As a matter of fact most leading Advertising Agencies offer this service and this, according to many experts, will be the buzz word of the nineties.

Thc pressure on retail shelves in urban markets has made it imperative for Marketers to look towards the rural markets for growth and survival. This is an area where tremendous potential exists. While companies like Hindustan Lever, ITC, etc. have made considerable inroads in this direction, a lot still needs to be done. That the nineties will see considerable work in this direction is beyond doubt.

The eighties was the watershed decade. It ushered in television, an affluent middle class and consequently a consumer boom. It led to a scramble by brands to get established. Much of the work started will come to fruition in the nineties. All in all, it promises to be an exciting decade for the Marketing Men.

12

Wooing Shelf Area for POP Display

Strategy for the Years to Come

P.K. SINHA

The trend in Indian marketing is towards POP promotion caused mainly due to the change in the buying behaviour towards impulse buying. Dr. Sinha in this paper outlines the way it is done and the practices prevalent. He talks mainly of Merchantising, a process of hiring mercenaries. He maintains that shelf area acquiring is key to success and ends with the comment that products that need Word-of-Mouth and the convenience products have to resort to this method of promotion.

— *EDITORS*

CONSUMERISM has arrived in India. The consumer, the king, is on the move. He is no more choiceless. The insurge in the consumer market has given the reins in the hands of the consumers and brand loyalty is starting to be a questionable behaviour. The noise in the media is reducing the chances of instant recall of specific brand by overcrowding the mind of the consumers. On a Sunday, when the consumer is relaxing and watching programmes on TV, is in a sense not at all relaxing. He is exposed to the highest noise level of the week. On that day itself, he is viewing no less than fifty ads on the TV itself, besides the print ads. The ads, instead of helping him decide, are, actually, making his life miserable. What does one do in such a case? The theory, that a customer comes to the market with a decision to buy a particular brand, is no more valid. In the consumer products, particularly the LIPS (Low Involvement Products), impulse buying is gaining the centre-stage. A recent study reveals that 38 per cent of the consumers buy on impulse (The value differing among the categories). The only way this phenomenon can be strategically exploited is through Point of Purchase (POP) displays. With competition growing stiff, this is the direction of marketing efforts. All large and keen competitors are trying to win the space in the shops.

The responsibility of POPs lies totally on the manufactures/marketeers. But, it requires full co-operation from the middlemen, both the wholesalers and the retailers. POP promotion consists of three major tasks, (a) preparing the display materials, like danglers, stickers, etc., (b) retailer motivation through citation, cash incentives, etc., and (c) acquiring shelf space for the company's products. Except the first, the other two are the responsibility of the sales representatives.

The retailers are classified into categories such as departmental stores, large retail outlets and small retailers. The company takes care of the departmental stores and large retailers and leaves the small retailers to be serviced by the wholesalers, keeping their number and variety in mind. The wholesalers exercise a good hold over the retailers because of their money power and the physical possession of the goods. Many retailers buy on credit and depend heavily on the wholesalers for timely delivery. In such a situation, a wholesaler enjoys a very strategic position with regard to the POP promotion. This is more true in small cities, where a single wholesaler services approximately 50 per cent of the retailers. In such a situation, the wholesaler is the decision maker for the retailers regarding displays, or pushing a particular brand. This has given rise to a phenomenon called *Merchantising*, wherein it is the merchant that is managed instead of the product. A merchantiser hires a task-force whose primary job is to get shelf space booked for the wholesaler and hence, the product. This task-force helps the retailers in displays and maintains a personal rapport with them. It assists the company regarding ensuring a proper display of the POP materials, rotating the products of the company, blocking the competitors' POP promotion and pass on the necessary information about consumer tastes and retailer grievances. This way they can be a very effective source of channel conflict reduction. The merchantisers come much more handy in the light of the fact that there is a huge number of retailers in this country making it almost impossible for the company sales force to give each of them a fair listening. The cost of such an exercise is forbidding. The only alternative is to depend on the wholesalers, even at the cost of losing some control of the channel. Sometimes this loss of control does lead to some unethical practices, such as, compelling the retailers to display only a specific brand, or even physical removal of the danglers of the competing brands. These practices, however, are attributed to the competition and the fact that it is the fittest and the strongest that stays ahead of others.

The shelf space is hired, generally on monthly basis and sometimes on quarterly basis. Companies like HLL, P & G, Nestle, etc. go for regular booking, whereas a few like FSL, Godrej, etc. use the space only in the case of a launch or when there has been an unforeseen change in sales. The rates of the display depend on the location of the shop, the place of display in the shop and the size of the display. The space in the shop is divided in three parts: the front lower and upper windows outside the shop, the front shelf inside the shop facing the entrance and the other shelves at eye level. The front shelf costs the highest as the chances of viewing is maximum.

The retailers get highly motivated in the event of a shelf display contest. This results in tremendous increase in sales, sometimes doubling. But, once the contest is over, the interest dampens and there is a considerable drop in sales. In any case, the displays give a good sales result. Retailers feel that this is as high as 50 per cent. It is also found that where the products like batteries, tea, biscuits, soaps, etc. benefit a lot by the displays, products like toothpastes, which are *taste* products, do not benefit much. It is, thus, the convenience products, which generate impulse buying, that should be given a chance for displays. The displays can also be very strategically used for launching a product which has to be given a high exposure and good Word-of-Mouth. Thus, even when the shelf displays involve a high cost, the trend in Indian buying is giving a way to this mode of promotion.

13

Bank Marketing : Emerging Challenges for 90s

RANJAN KUMAR BAL

Banks have always been the target of criticism. The reason being the level of interaction with the public which no other institution commands. A vast network of banks have emerged, particularly after nationalization, playing their roles in national development. But their performances have always been questioned. The catch lies with Customer Service. Prof. Bal, in this paper, attempts to find out the ways to achieve this. In the process, he points out the challenges before the banking sector in the decade to come. He indicates that banks are no more restricted to a particular class of people. It is now **mass** banking. Even the lending base has shifted from assets to production. Indian banks have made laudable progress, but in customer service they lag far behind their foreign counterparts. The solution to all these problems, the author suggests, lies in the development of marketing as an organizational philosophy.

An alarming problem the banks face today is the decrease of the household savings and its routing to other competing companies like UTI, LIC, Post Offices, and other *Patras* floated by the government, besides the private banks. The banks can no more afford to sit and watch. They have to find a way out. Quickly. Some of the openings suggested by Prof. Bal are rural areas, improvement in technology and using the STP formulae : Segment, Target and Position. He concludes with the message that a proactive and deliberate effort to identify customer needs and develop ways to satisfy them is the only solution for a face-lift of the banks.

— *EDITORS*

BANKS act as the catalysts in India's planning efforts to bring about a rapid, purposive and significant change in the development of agriculture and industry. The public sector banks accounting for more than 90 per cent of the total bank deposits, are always called upon to play a developmental role and assist the government in the implementation of socio-economic programmes.

The period after 1969 has seen a complete transformation of Indian banking from **class** banking to **mass** banking. This period also witnessed unprecedented qualitative and quantitative changes in Indian banking which gave rise to numerous challenges. During coming years, the success of the banking sector will depend upon its ability to effectively meet the emerging challenges.

There is a general misconception that marketing is more relevant in production-oriented business of tangible goods and not in a service-oriented industry like banking. But in today's competitive banking world, marketing is becoming increasingly necessary. "Banking sector is probably the most important financial sector, not just in term of turnover, profit and employment, but also in its paramount impact on the other spheres of the economy. For these reasons, in the last few years, there has been a growing interest in applying marketing techniques and tools in the field of banking"[1].

The present article has been divided into four parts. In the first part, marketing's role in banking has been discussed. The second part examines the changing face of Indian banking. The third part presents the Indian banking scenario. The last part deals with the challenges for the marketing of banking services in 90s.

Marketing's Role in Banking

Bank marketing is the creation and delivery of financial

services suitable to meet the customers' needs at a profit to the bank. Two important functions of bank marketing are to attract and mobilise deposits on one hand and attract borrowers and users of services on the other. The importance of marketing approach in the banking sector stems from the intense competition not only from other banks, but also from financial corporation, post offices, and insurance companies. The need also arises due to sophistication of the bank customers, improvement in work technology and increased cost of meeting customers' needs. A way of thinking along marketing lines is essential in all areas of banking to enable the bank to match its resources with customer requirements in the most profitable manner. The following model, developed by Arthur Meiden[2], shows the marketing approach to banking services.

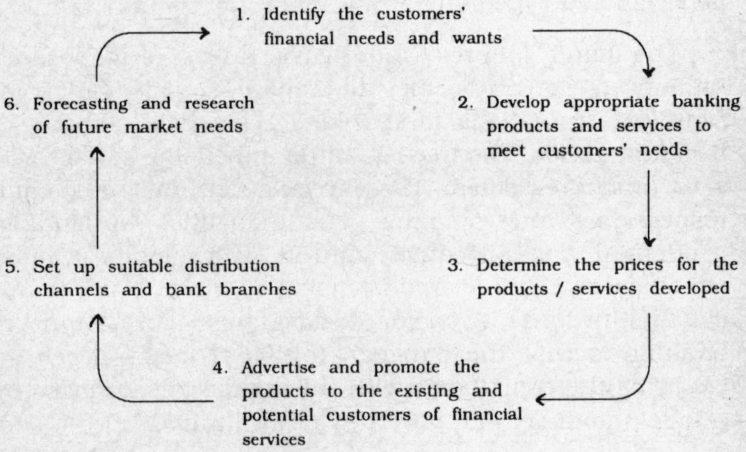

The Changing Face of Indian Banking

During the last two decades, Indian banking has undergone revolutionary changes. Apart from unprecedented growth and functional diversification, there has, in fact, been a change in the concept, precept and outlook of banking.[3] The post-independence era witnessed a complete transformation of Indian banking from "class" banking to "mass" banking, from "asset-based" lending to "production - oriented" lending and from "elite" banking to "social" banking. Analysing the history of Indian banking, we can identify four types of banking which have evolved over a period of time.[4]

(i) Banking as Business Deals

When Britishers came to India, they brought along with them the type of commercial banking that was practised in London. In this type of banking there is a close relationship between the businessman and the banker and the bank lending is based on confidentiality and a personal equation.

(ii) Regulated Banking

The bank failures and heavy losses of depositors influenced the authorities to impose a wide variety of stringent regulations for banking. This type of banking began in 1930s. The freedom of the practising banker was very much restricted. These regulations included bank inspections, interest rates, conditionalities in lending, prudential and allocative controls over credits, capital adequacy regulations and licensing of banking and financial institutions.[5] A major disadvantage of this type of banking is that the banker's role is reduced largely to ensuring the compliance with the regulations imposed by central monetary and government authorities.

(iii) Developmental Banking

After nationalisation of major commercial banks in 1969, this third type of banking emerged in India. Consequently, the banking network spread quickly and the progress in deposit mobilisation and credit allocation has been remarkable. Banks have played an important role in the implementation of the socio-economic programmes for raising economic standards of people. In the development of agriculture and industry their role is praise-worthy.

(iv) Market-Oriented Banking

This phase in banking started in the early eighties in India. The new trend of disintermediation and high degree of competition contributed to the development of this kind of banking. As the needs, attitudes and preferences of customers are changing, banks need to adopt a market-oriented approach, if they have to increase, or even maintain their deposit/lending base.

Although the above four types of banking have evolved in India, in practice, we find only the mixed types.

Indian Banking Scenario

Marketing came into banks in the late 1950s, not in the form of the marketing concept, but in the form of advertising and promotion.[6] In India, however, the importance in banking was realised much later. The first major step in this direction was initiated by the State Bank of India in 1972 when it reorganized itself on the basis of major market segments. Four major segments were created: small industries and small businesses, agriculture, commercial and institutional, and personal and service banking.[7] The organizational structure of the bank has been redesigned to accommodate the market segmentation approach.

In the early 1980s, banks started thinking in terms of product development, market penetration and market development.[8] Banks also accelerated their process of equipping their staff with the marketing capabilities in terms of both skills and attitudes through different training programmes. At present, banks in India provide over 50 services to their customers in various forms ranging from different deposit accounts and credit schemes to ancillary services and consultancy services in addition to international trade facilities.[9] However, we are still lagging far behind the services rendered by the banks of the developed countries. In the U.K., banks offer over 120 individual services. Banks in the U.S.A. render 350 financial products to its customers. Even foreign banks in India offer many innovative financial services, including the services of electronic gadgets, automatic teller machines, etc., that enable customers to perform basic operations round the clock. Indian Banks organise **"credit melas"** to market the advances at public functions by explaining the details of advances disbursed.

There is a wide spread feeling that the quality in customer service, specially in the urban areas, is deteriorating. Although 1986 was declared as the "Year of Customer", no perceptible development was noticed. The national survey[10] of savers conducted by the National Institute of Bank Management found that majority of savers were more or less satisfied with the services of the banks. But, by taking a positive approach towards the opinions of the non-committal bank savers, we can say that there is ample scope for further improvement in banking services. Searching for the reasons for deterioration we find that tremendous increase in the quantitative dimensions caused an enormous strain on the banks in terms of manpower, infrastructural facilities, systems and procedures, and management capabilities leading to customer services falling short of expectations. Development of marketing as an organisational philosophy would enable banks to understand the needs of the customers better and devise means and ways to respond to these needs.

It is noticed that the rate of growth in bank deposits has not matched the growth in the domestic saving rate. This means that the surplus generated in the economy is being diverted to other forms of savings. Between 1983-84 and 1985-86, the share of bank deposits in total household savings in the form of financial assets declined from 50 per cent to 47 per cent. This shows the erosion of the popularity of the banks in the household sector. The lack of marketing is one of the main reasons.

There is lack of marketing culture in the Indian banks. Creative and innovative banking is impeded due to the rigid regulatory framework imposed on the banking system. The regulatory measures of the Reserve Bank of India and the Government of India reduce the lendable resources for innovative banking. There is dirth of appropriate incentives for successful marketing activities.

Challenges for the 90s

During the coming years, banks will face tough competition from government agencies as well as private and public corporate sector in mobilising savings. As the tempo of branch expansion has reduced considerably, it appears difficult for the banks to maintain the present growth rate during 1990s. "The emergence of a number of mutual funds, introduction of a variety of new saving schemes with tax concessions by UTI, floating of convertible and non-convertible debentures by companies of a high credit rating, higher interest rates on company deposits, better resource management by the corporate sectors are likely to take away a large volume of funds from the banking system which will affect the deposit growth rate of commercial banks in the remaining years of the century".[11] Thus, the days of wait business for the banks are over. The present trends reveal possibly an alarming future situation for banking industry on the deposit mobilisation front. In future years, the bankers will have to be after the customers and offer schemes to meet their needs.

The mounting overdues of banks have become a cause of serious concern, which is a great danger to the health of the banking sector. This trend continuing during 1990s, it would seriously affect the ability of the banking system to recycle scarce resources.

Much of the future relating to Indian banks lies in the rural areas. While rural branches account for 57 per cent of the total branch network, the share of rural deposits is a meagre 14 per cent. Much remains to be achieved both in terms of mobilising resources and marketing a wide range of banking facilities in the rural area. The Service Area Approach to rural lending, which became operational from 1st April, 1989, is a major step to improve the quality of rural lending. The 90s will reveal the effectiveness of this approach in meeting the appropriate credit needs of the rural people.

The Planning Commission in its final approach paper has proposed average annual growth target of 5.5 per cent during Eighth Plan and 3 per cent in employment over the decade. These targets would require an averge rate of domestic saving of around 2.5 per cent. Banks have a major role to play in achieving this required saving rate.

The coming years are likely to witness many technologically advanced industries coming into existence. Banks have to develop expertise to facilitate technical appraisal on proper lines. The alarming problem of industrial sickness, especially in the small scale sector, is a cause of great concern for the banks. The banks need to strengthen not only their loan appraisal system, but also their monitoring mechanism so as to get timely signals of sickness.

To cope with the rapid expansion in the geographical coverage and business, structural changes in the banking industry setup will have to be considered and the banking industry will have to be restructured to improve the efficiency of banking operations and to promote their active participation in the process of development.[12] As there is no unique way to restructuring the organisation, it would require a lot of thinking and conceptual inputs from the experts and the top level executives of banks during the coming years.

Improvement in work technology will lead to improvement of the quality of customer service, house-keeping, controls and managerial functions. A state has already been reached when use of mechanical and electronic aids, in order to serve the customer as he rightly expects to be served, can not be deferred any longer. Fears of the employees about the effects of the computers have to be dispelled and they should be taken into confidence for creating a good climate in the organisation, so that computerisation will be successful.[13]

One of the major findings of the national level survey conducted by National Institute of Bank Management is that, banking is largely a habit of literate Indian citizens (86 to 94 per cent of bank savers). However, a majority (30 to 42 per cent) of the non-bank savers are illiterate. Hence, proper marketing strategies to exploit this potential market for deposits are necessary. It is also a challenge for banks to develop innovative schemes to attract production workers and young savers (below the age of 30) who are potential bank depositors.

The level of awareness about bank deposit schemes are quite low among non-bank savers. Some existing schemes of banks, e.g., cash certificates are not widely known by even bank savers. The National Institute of Bank Management survey also shows that a sizeable portion of bank savers are ignorant about mail and telegraphic transfer facilities provided by banks. Thus, appropriate promotional strategy to make the schemes more popular is an essential step to penetrate the hitherto untapped market.

The banks need to study carefully the various segments of the population and formulate appropriate schemes to suit those specific requirements. Bhattacharya and Bose[14] present the segmentwise marketing strategy in the following table, which is worth mentioning here.

Segmentwise Marketing Strategy

Segments	Appropriate Product for the Potential Market Segments	Strategy
Households		
a) Small savers in semi-urban and rural areas specially agriculturists, production workers and young generation.	a) Deposit schemes with door to door and at the working place collection facility (specially for production workers) b) New innovative location specific credit/deposit schemes satisfying motives behind savings. c) Mutual Funds d) Rural Credit Cards	a) Significant promotional campaign by personal contact, preferably through commission agents
b) Professional and service workers.	a) Deposit and credit schemes with high liquidity and instant payment facility anywhere in India. b) Consumer durables finance scheme with a package of items depending on disposable income of the customers. c) Credit Cards, etc.	a) Promotion by mail shot, telephone calls, customer meets, hoardings. b) Personalised customer service
c) Retired and about to be retired persons.	a) Monthly or bi-monthly interest payable deposit schemes with post-dated interest warrants payable anywhere in India.	a) Contacting this segment just before retirement by collecting lists from their respective organisations b) Quality customer service to them with due respect and courtesy

d) High income metropolitian customers.	a) Deposit scheme with ATM facilities b) Tax consultation c) Portfolio management d) consumer finance e) credit cards, etc	a) Special cadre marketing officers to be created to contact this segment at clubs, offices, etc. b) Perservice c) Promotion through telephone calls, greeting cards, etc.
e) Housewives.	a) Deposit schemes at the door b) Special credit schemes for unemployed house wives	a) Special female marketing officers or female commission agents b) Campaign through female voluntary agencies
Institutions		
a) Large corporate industrial/commercial sector	a) New product like commercial paper b) Suitable form of zero-coupon bonds and warrants c) Corporate credit cards d) Working capital loan with pre assigned yearly credit limits for next five years e) Broad-based merchant banking f) International borrowing facilities, etc.	a) Special commercial branch with motivated and specially trained staff to handle these customers b) Promotion through periodic visits to top executives of corporate sector
b) Medium and small size industrial / commercial sector	a) Factoring b) Financial Counselling c) Management Consultancy d) Tax Consultancy e) Special counters and branches and staff for dealing exclusively for particular type of industry.	a) Specialised marketing officers to deal exclusively with this segment b) Promotion through customer education and increasing awareness of different existing and new services

... *Contd.* ...

	f) Aggressive selling of existing credit related products like card, bill discounting, export, import, finance, guarantees, etc.	
	g) Credit Cards	
c) Rural Industry	a) Location specific credit scheme b) Rural Credit Card c) Agricultural / Industrial Consultancy Centres (one centre per 300 villages)	a) Promotion through continuous interaction in the management of their industry

Conclusion

In the present environment, bankers operatc in a "buyers' market". As they are at the mercy of the customers, there is need for application of planned marketing approach to find proper outlets for banking services. Deliberately initiating the marketing process to convert systematically identified target groups of potential customers into actual customers deserves all necessary attention.

The future of banking lies in identifying customer needs and developing new ways for satisfying their needs. For this purpose imaginative and innovative changes are essential and marketing is the key to these changes. Bankers have to study the motives, habits, feelings and preferences of their customers if they are to become truely marketing oriented. We hope, during 90s, the banks will follow an aggressive marketing approach to improve their performances in all fronts.

REFERENCES

1. Meiden, Arthur, *Bank Marketing Management*, MacMillan Studies in Marketing Management, 1984, p. 1.
2. Ibid., p. 16.
3. Ghose, B.K., "Bank Nationalisation - Promises and Performance", *The Journal of Indian Institute of Bankers*, July-Sept., 1987, p. 126.
4. Singh, Sampat P. "Future of Indian Banking", *NIBM* Working Papers, 1987, p. 1.
5. Ibid., p. 4.
6. Kotler, Philip, *Marketing Management : Analysis, Planning and Control* Prentice-Hall, 1980, p. 12.
7. Joshi, N.C., "Relevance of Marketing Strategies in Banks", *The Economic Times*, Bombay, March 17, 1988, p. 7.
8. Saxena K.K., *Bank Marketing : Concepts & Applications*, Skylark Publications, New Delhi, 1988, p. 11.
9. Singh, Ajit, "Training for Bank Marketing", *Financial Express*, Bombay, Dec. 31, 1986, p. 6.
10. Rao, V.K.B., "Marketing of Bank Services", *Indian Journal of Marketing*, Sept. 1986, p. 24.
11. National Institute of Bank Management. "All India Savings and Deposit Trends and Patterns", 1986, *Highlights*, p. 34.
12. Power, B.B., *Indian Banking Profile for 1990s.*
13. Saha, Kakoli, "Computerisation in Banks : Implications for Organisational Development", *Vikalpa*, July-Sept., 1986, p. 236.
14. Bhattacharya, B.N. and Ghose, B.K., "Marketing of Banking Services in the 90s : Problems and Perspectives", *Economic and Political Weekly*, Feb. 25, 1989.

14

Ecological Perspectives of Marketing in the 1990s :

Conserver Marketing for Sustainable Development

ATUL PARVATIYAR

Dr. Parvatiyar in this paper is trying to look into the role marketing can play in conservation : The need of every country. Deforestation, excessive use of finite energy sources and polluting and wasteful production have given a comfortable life to the human beings. But it is only material aspect of it. It has, on the other hand, made the life difficult by making the environment impure. In such a situation a concept of sustainable development has to be put forward for all industries and human beings too. 1990s will see a thrust in this regard. The main cause for such a situation is scarcity. Pondering on this issue, this paper raises and answers three questions : Will this scarcity have any impact on marketing, will the public support this view of conservation and also the organisations that take up such jobs and what actions should the companies take to achieve this.

Working on these lines, the author indicates that scarcity will make marketing more socially responsible. He analyses the opportunities and threats attached to such environmental issues and suggests that cycling of wastes and changing of consumption patterns will be the main areas of action besides thinking in the line of introducing socio-ecological products. He concludes the paper with a note that marketing can play a rewarding role in conserver society but it will require a cohesive effort from the managers and academia. It has to be given a different perspective than just a fad for rich intellectuals.

— *EDITORS*

Printed with permission from the Editor, *Management and Labour Studies*, a quarterly journal of Xavier Labour Relations Institute, Jamshedpur where this paper was first published.

MARKETING professionals must be prepared to meet a new challenge in an era of increased public concern over environmental deterioration, resource shortages, explosive population growth, world hunger and poverty.

Hundreds of organizations and individuals representing our society expressed their common concerns for the human environment in their appearance and submissions before the World Commission on Environment and Development (WCED 1987). Indications are that in the coming decade, the global slogan will be "Sustainable Development" giving further impetus to the conserver movement. This will have far reaching implications for the development of global economic systems and for political actions affecting the nature of marketing.

Promoting a conserver ethos is both socially desirable and a perceived ecological necessity. The management of environmental resources is necessary to ensure sustainable human progress and even human survival. A secular trend towards shortage of materials and increasing environmental decay can only be altered by a new understanding of economic growth, one that must be based on policies that sustain and expand the environmental resource base. Marketing's challenge will be to meet this human need. Marketing managers, accustomed to gear production and distribution strategies to the never-ending growth of demand for their products and a limitless supply of resources may view such concerns with mixed feelings. They have generally emphasized the demand aspect of marketing to the neglect of important supply issues. Marketing not only needs to adjust to this environment, but to develop a proactive, entrepreneurial orientation to the management of the external environment (Zeithaml and Zeithaml, 1984).

Conserverism and Sustainable Development

The organized conserver movement[1] for the protection and enhancement of the living environment of the people advocates a change in the orientation of economic growth. They favour growth that is forceful and at the same time socially and environmentally sustainable for the benefit of future generations (WCED, 1987). They challenge the conventional methods of measuring 'economic growth' by Gross National Product or per capita national income which only reflect the "forward through put" in a production-to-consumption pipeline. Their focus is on beneficial 'forward through put', wherein adequate attention at the beginning of the pipeline is ensured so that resources used for production of goods do not damage the environment (Shapiro 1978).

Adopting a philosophy of sustainable development, the conserverists are critical of any marketing approach which aims at serving the material wants of consumers through an ever increasing volume of goods without any attempt to maximize life quality (Kotler, 1988). Now, life quality represents not only the quantity and quality of consumer goods and services but also the quality of the environment. Modern marketing techniques like advertising, which artificially encourage the ever-growing per capita demand for consumer goods, have been questioned by protagonists of conserver societies (Shapiro, 1978).

The message is loud and clear. Exponential economic growth will not continue indefinitely, unless resources are conserved, pollution abated and population checked. Thus the emphasis has to be placed on the characteristics and side effects of growth, rather than on its mere existence or absence.

Marketing in a Situation of Sustainable Development

Marketing plays a role in the development process by

offering consumption opportunities to satisfy human needs and wants. It identifies real and perceived needs in the context of the social and cultural environment to which it adjusts its offerings. However, marketing's critical role in development will be appreciated only when it meets the needs of the present without compromising the ability of future generations to meet their own needs.

Marketing must contribute in meeting the essential needs of the world's poor and pay attention to such considerations as changes in the access to resources and in the distribution of costs and benefits. The importance of marketing as an essential developmental activity to achieve many objectives of the Less Developed Countries have been stressed by many marketing scholars (Kinsey, 1982; Kotler, 1986; Riley; 1983; Dholakia, 1984; and Carter, 1986). Yet the marketing issues related to the promotion of values that encourage sustainable development by promoting consumption standards which respect ecological perspectives have received scant attention.[2]

Not all marketers would agree that such issues deserve the attention of the discipline and of the fraternity. They would argue that mankind, through its ability to innovate and substitute, has quickly overcome scarcities in the past. Another line of argument could be that many essential human needs can be met only through goods and services provided by industry. And marketing's job is limited to offering products and services that could serve such needs. If the production of goods requires increasing amounts of agrochemicals and machinery, marketing has to make these available. Marketing must provide the material basis of contemporary standards of living. It will change its offerings with changes in the material needs of society that might accompany environmental changes.

On the other hand, there are also marketers who are concerned with scarcities, pollution, environmental conservation and the poverty and hunger of a larger multitude of the human race. However, even these would raise some fundamental questions related to the adoption of any conserver marketing policy.

(i) Will scarcities really have any impact on marketing? If yes, what would be the nature of the impact?

(ii) How would the general masses view such concern for ecology and the need for conservation of resources? Will there be enough consumers to support organizations that adopt a conserver approach?

(iii) What type of corporate marketing actions are appropriate to this philosophy?

My attempt in what follows is to resolve some of these issues and present a typology for global conserver marketing action.

Impact of Scarcities and Conserverism on Marketing

In a state of resource shortage what is likely to be the impact on the marketing function? Considering that many scarcities are permanent rather than temporary, the possible consequences would be that :

(i) Scarcities are likely to alter the speed, direction and motivation of economic growth.[3]

(ii) They are likely to impact upon life-styles, moving demand away from those products and services which are materials- wasteful, energy-intensive or nature-polluting.

(iii) Scarcities are likely to produce inflation in a world where poverty and inequity are endemic, and, therefore, likely to distort certain demand patterns[4].

(iv) Scarcities will require recuperation and recycling of waste generated in the consumption process together with efforts aimed at enhancing the resource base for sustainable development.

(v) Scarcities will thoroughly modify the task of advertising and distribution.

(vi) Scarcities are likely to give rise to conserver societies which would plead for full cost pricing incorporating all relevant factors[5], so that the market system could allocate resources in a manner that more closely reflects societal needs both immediate and long-term.

(vii) Firms using increasingly scarce minerals would face substantial cost increases. They may not find it easy to pass these cost increase on to consumers.

(viii) Energy prices are likely to be unstable, given the shortage and depletion of most finite, non-renewable sources of energy. Buying patterns may considerably change due to changing energy costs and the consequent search for alternative sources of energy.

(ix) Marketers may face, in many developing countries at least, increased government regulation and intervention directed towards conservation. These would make marketing more constrained and socially responsible (Parvatiyar, 1988a). Such regulation may also provide opportunities for those in marketing of pollution control devices and in exploration and research directed towards discovering new sources of energy or suitable substitutes.

(x) In a condition of permanent scarcities, the task of consumer behaviour specialists gets modified. While investigating consumer behaviour, these specialists have till now accepted without question the credo *more is better* and a basic assumption of effective insatiability of human wants. It is only by exception that efforts are made to pass judgment on the relative merits of the different products and services being assessed by the consumer. More attention will have to be focussed on exploring consumer behaviour in the perspective of the public concern for sustainable development.

Global Conserver Ethos in the 1990s

The emerging global realization is that many of the development paths followed by nations are clearly unsustainable. Society cannot afford to waste resources. This is especially so in the developing countries, which already find themselves in a situation of scarcity. Urgent action has to be taken to improve the environment of these countries. Often this means action rather than the stoppage of action. But in the wake of resources constraints and the inability of these nations to invest large sums of money, the only available public policy option involves *'doing more with less'*.

The developed countries, too, are realizing that links exist between poverty, inequality, and environmental degradation to which they are vulnerable. Hence, the strategic imperatives of the 1990s for the developed countries are to foster a growth revival in the developing countries. Such development decisions undertaken by industrialised countries will have a profound effect on the global trading and marketing environment.

Thus it would be appropriate as a global policy to remove some of the trade barriers against the export of manufactured goods from developing countries so that these nations are not forced to trade mainly commodities and minerals to the industrialized countries to finance their imports. In order to sustain the high growth rate needed in developing countries, vulnerable sections of the population such as farmers and small producers have to be protected from being marginalized. The continuation of subsidies on agriculture in developed countries, affecting international prices, will increase the pressure on farmers in developing countries to over-exploit natural resources to maintain their income.

Another policy appropriate to the conserver approach would be full cost pricing. Such a pricing policy requires the inclusion of the cost of impact on the environment produced by a manufacturing project into the price at which goods are offered in the market. The pricing mechanism should reflect not only the private cost but also the total cost to society including the net energy used, the ecological impact, and other social considerations. Environmental impact assessment studies could form the basis for computing the cost of these externalities.

An urgent global task would be to enhance the resource base primarily to relieve pressure on the use of land, water, and livestock. This would require an increase in productivity based on a controlled and more efficient application of water and agrochemicals, the extensive use of organic manures and of non-chemical means of pest control. Productivity can also increase by scientific afforestation, waste land development, water management and aquaculture. These alternatives can be promoted only by an agricultural policy based on ecological realities (WCED, 1987).

Finally, a reform of inefficient consumption habits would make it much easier to do more with less. Wasteful energy consumption pollutes the biosphere and eats into scarce fossil fuel supplies. A reduction in the per capita consumption of energy and a shift to non-polluting technologies and sources of energy will have to be achieved. In this regard, the use of social marketing techniques might prove far more effective than either governmental flats or pious exhortations. Changing consumption patterns will call for new policies in urban development, industry location, housing design, transportation systems, and the choice of agricultural and industrial technologies.

Corporate Strategies in Conserver Marketing

Corporate strategies for conserver marketing have to be built on enlightened self interest, so that ecologically responsible marketing opportunities are sought for (Drucker, 1984; Robin and Reidenbach, 1987). Marketing has to be linked to the opportunities and threats in production-consumption process affecting environmental issues such as:

(i) Depletion of natural resources;

(ii) Disposal of pollution producing wastes;

(iii) Despoliation of the environment; and

(iv) Energy inputs and costs.

Exhibit – I illustrates the marketing opportunities and threats linked to environmental problems in several cases. It shows that opportunities are available to marketers to change the end-product mix or improve technologies so as to reduce the input of physical resources per crore of rupees worth of output, or to increase the re-use of the inputs. Unless such opportunities are used, the resulting increase in environmental problems will lead to a threat of public boycott, mandatory actions or regulations imposed by government. Such situations have already been seen in the 1980s, when a significant number of organizations faced active opposition from protest groups against their marketing policies (Garett, 1987). Chakraborty (1988) on the basis of a detailed case study of 'The Doon Valley Experience' concludes that when no safer substitutes for a hazardous product is known to a marketer, the course of action will be to resolve the conflict by working the trade-offs. Such solutions are temporary and leave a residual risk.

Marketing perspectives will, therefore, have to change from a reactive approach to a proactive, entrepreneurial orientation to the management of the external environment. The corporate body cannot afford to rest content with managing the consequences of events that have taken place. It would be doomed if it specializes in managing the aftermath (Ghosh, 1988). Every corporate entity has to see itself as an economic agent for accelerating the process of development.

EXHIBIT — I

Illustration of Marketing Opportunities and Threats Under Different Environmental Problems

	Problems of Environment			
	Depletion of natural resources	*Disposal of wastes with concurrent pollution*	*Despollation of the environment*	*Energy inputs and costs*
Opportunities	• Development of new sources or substitutes	• Energy generation from waste and recycling process	• New Industries based on biotechnology	• Development of new technology
	• Opportunities for fine ceramics, rare metals, metal alloys, and high performance plastics	• Savings in costs on scarce inputs by recycling of products	• Agrochemical industries	• Use of alternative sources of energy in product operation or production process
	• Products improving productivity of present systems	• Recycling centres	• Pollution control equipment like scrubbers, etc.	• Efficient products in terms of energy consumption
	• Technologies improving agricultural resource base like high yield crop varieties, wasteland development, pest control measures	• Alternative packaged goods	• Subsidies on manufacture and marketing of ecologically benign products	• Efficient living environment
	• Agriculture service equipment like those for weather forecasting, storage and transport	• Packaging material based on biodegradable products	• Development of new industrial process	• Information technology for productivity, energy, and resource efficiency
	• Acquaculture	• Reusable products	• Health products based on	• New energy bases

	• Water resource management	• Opportunity for high-tech products to clean oil slick and space equipment • Detergents based on biodegradable products	genetic engineering • Marketing of parks and packaged environments	like plants as substitute to fossil fuel
Threats	• Ban on use of certain resources as raw material for manufacturing products	• Public action and poor image	• Regulatory measures on reducing emission	• Reduced consumer preference for products having high energy input costs
	• Substantial cost increases due to high cost extraction	• Restrictions on new increase in capacity	• Pollution charges	• Ban or increased taxes on use of fossil fuel
	• Change in consumer demand towards ecologically benign products	• Governmental regulation and tax disadvantage	• Ban on usage of chemical pollutants	• Unstable international prices
	• Technological obsolescence and competition from substitute products	• Compensation claims • Legal action	• Public action and conflict situations • Action against deforesters high-rise builders	
	• Regulation on use of forest based products		• Legal and governmental action against manufacturers of hazardous health products • Restriction on marketing and advertising.	

How do corporate marketers cope with this problem? The foremost involvement of marketing in the conserver approach is to diversify demand away from products and services which are materials-wasteful and energy intensive. But into what? That is the crux of the matter. It is one thing to entice the owners of motor vehicles to acquire more compact models, reduce their cruising speed, or travel in car pools. It is quite something else to research, develop, and market those products and services which absorb the purchasing power freed by the reduction of waste — and in the process to expand the overall economy. A similar dilemma arises when people are motivated not to cut trees though there is no other source of fuel; or save power when most of the household appliances are electrically operated.

The Socio-ecological Product

Marketing which believes in innovation as its prime strategy will have to concentrate on developing socio-ecological products. This is a concept suggesting that environmental consequences and the product's aggregate impact on everyone affected by its acceptability than either user satisfaction or corporate profitability (Cracco and Rostenne, 1971).

Firms in the small and medium sectors could look for options in the use of new technologies and production processes, with the help of micro-electronics, which would reduce production costs. Energy-saving biological systems may well be suited to the needs of these firms for pollution control or waste disposal.

Small and medium firms which constitute the largest segment of industry in most nations need information, which can help improve productivity and energy and resource efficiency. Appropriate market information would help them target their market offerings, involving minimum waste and lowest energy costs.

(ii) Recycling : A Strategic Marketing Choice

Under the conserver ethos, waste management issues will rank very high. Marketing mix variables could be strategically used by corporate marketers to gain favourable public opinion. Firms engaged in recycling activities, the creation of packaged environments (Parvatiyar, 1988), the distribution of recovered wastes, the maintenance and conservation of public utilities, the enhancement of resources, and customer education are likely to benefit in the conserver society.

Recycling, through the use of reverse channels of distribution, as in the case of waste paper, soft drink bottles and aluminium, copper, and brass utensils in India, assures the marketer of both favourable conserverist support and raw materials at low prices. Consumers, too, see tangible monetary benefits in the process of waste recycling and this will influence the choices they make.

An excellent example of how a multifaceted marketing opportunity through waste processing was gainfully exploited, is the case of Sulabh International. It has not only successfully marketed the concept of low cost public toilets, but has also used the human waste to produce and market electricity and fertilizers. Intensive-spatial distribution and the clean hygienic environment of the public toilets are factors contributing to the considerable national and international success of the organisation in less than 12 years of its inception (Parvatiyar 1986). This substantiates our hypothesis that a socio-ecological product would have a great potential for market expansion.

(iii) Changing Consumer Bias

There are still important tasks for corporate conserver marketing. It must accept a macro, or societal concept of demarketing (Rotenberg, 1975), rather than the customary micro-approach (Kotler and Levy. 1971). Consumer bias towards satisfying wants through indiscriminate consumption must be changed and wasteful consumption habits discouraged. Marketing's role in a world of resource shortages is to promote their more efficient use and to teach consumers how to derive greater satisfaction from consuming less. The use of advertising and other forms of marketing communication will help marketers educate consumers in the proper use of higher quality socio-ecological products, even though their initial costs may be somewhat high.

Corporate strategies to maintain public property such as gardens, parks, and other public utility centres have spin-off benefits in corporate image building. Companies could gain substantially more in generating a favourable image if they undertook activities related to the enhancement of the resources base, the encouragement of small firms, research and development on environmental issues, and the introduction of pollution control and waste treatment facilities.

Finally, firms must recognize the ecological and resource recovery impact of what they market. If the marketing concept means consumer satisfaction with the goods and services offered, it also includes the movement, recovery and generation of resources to produce the goods and services. If renewable ecological resources are to be economically used, then as part of the corporate strategy, the renewing activity must be at least double the extracting activity. For example, forest based industries as well as the people using forest resources must meet their needs by planting trees for fuel, fodder, and commercial timber.

Business firms have to tie in the environmental impact and various raw material alternatives to such elements as company objectives, financing, consumer needs and government constraints. Business and technology will need to turn to new directions, away from the ideal of quantity growth and towards an emphasis on quality, after sale service, durability, conservation of materials and economy and efficiency in the use of energy.

A Typology of Conserver Marketing Actions

Exhibit – II purports to depict broad categories of marketing action based on Galbraith's three-part framework (Galbraith, 1977). The framework has been modified to include different levels of marketing environment stimulators. The framework does not purport to be an exhaustive list of conserver marketing actions, nor does it develop new strategies. It is only intended to provide a perspective through which a proactive, entrepreneurial orientation can be developed.

The Exhibit contains examples of strategic, cooperative or independent conserver marketing actions that may be undertaken by international associations, national governments of industrialized and developing countries, marketers, public and voluntary organisations and educators.

EXHIBIT – II follows . . .

EXHIBIT — II

Types of Conserver Marketing Action

Level of marketing environment stimulators	*Independent action*	*Strategic action*	*Cooperative action*
International Association	• Incentives and grant-in-aid to ecologically benign products • Economic efficiency measures to encourage internationalization of environmental costs	• Policy and measures favouring exports from developing countries • International economic adjustment • Institutional reforms	• Common mandates on sustainable development • Develop a common code of conduct
Industrialised Countries	• Measures on pollution control and conservation of resources • Regulations and policies favouring industries with conservational approaches • Maintenance and development plans on ecosystem • Institutional and legal changes	• Allow financial flows to developing countries • Lending for sustainable development • Removal of subsidies from agricultural production • Reduce protectionism to manufactured products of LDCs • Build up technological base in LDCs	• Multilateral trade agreements • Develop common pricing policy • Common code of conduct on use of pollution intensive goods • Assist in cooperative research and development projects • Set-up joint ventures on conserver projects with other countries
Less Developed Countries	• Regulations and taxes for efficient use of energy and raw materials • Broadened environmental assessment policies • Subsidies to promote ecologically benign products • Population control measures • Enhancing renewable resource base	• Land reforms and integrated rural development • Expand technological base and measures to improve productivity • Institutional reforms • Urban development policy	• Cooperation with developed countries on technological upgradation • Joint research projects • Bilateral and multilateral trade agreements for reducing commodity exports • Cooperation in space and sea research programmes

Industry	• Utilise opportunities in ecologically benign products • Change technologies and technological processes • Broaden environment assessments • Improve productivity	• Research and development in new and useful technologies • Change structure of world industry • Industrialization efforts in the Third World • Establish environmental goals • Worker training	• Develop common code of conduct • International trade association set standards • Encourage joint research • Industry seminars
Marketing Educator	• Inclusion of conserver approaches in course curriculum • Researches on consumer behaviour under conserverism • Publish articles and books favouring conserver action	• Set-up centres for study on conserver marketing • Consumer education on conservation • Sections on conserver approaches in journals	• Undertake consultancy on conserver marketing approaches • Hold conferences and seminars

Nature of Consumer Research in Conserver Marketing

The basic question in advocating a conserver corporate marketing approach is : how will consumers react to this approach? Will customers pay more for the socio-ecological product? How many customers will be willing to pay more? Also, what percentage of the privileged class will be prepared to reduce their standard of living, as it is customarily understood, so that resources may be either preserved for future generations or be made available to less fortune populations? Are there any distinct characteristic differences among ecologically concerned consumers and ecologically indifferent consumers ?

Such questions are valid expressions of concern of marketing practitioners that have to be explored by marketing academicians and researchers. There have been some micro-level studies, but they are related to a specific product or brand.[6] We may cite the success stories of specific ecologically benign products to justify our stand in proposing a conserver marketing approach, but, we have also to state honestly that macro level research to answer such questions is lacking.

We conjecture, with the above disclaimer, that in the 1990s there will be a substantial groups of consumers, both in India and in other countries, who would be ecologically more conscious and conserver oriented. The logic supporting this conjecture is that the 1970s and 1980s have witnessed the inclusion of environmental studies in primary and secondary school curricula. Thus, generations conscious of environmental issues are likely to be in decision-making positions in the 1990s.

Nevertheless, we must admit that academic researchers have not effectively addressed themselves to the intensive study of the all important ecological factors in our research on purchasing decisions. Instead of directing the total focus of our discipline and multivariate techniques and buyer seller interactions in consumer behaviour models, we must relate marketing to the larger system and our research must be oriented in that direction.

Conclusion — The Need for Collegial Action

Instead of conserverism remaining an upper middle class concern or a fad among relatively well to do intellectuals, the task of the marketing fraternity is to teach consumers how to buy so as to help conserve energy and dwindling resources. Marketing know-how used to change consumer perspectives toward conservation, will make the marketing discipline more relevant. For, relevance means relating the discipline to societal goals. Bottom line thinking that plugs in only to company self-preservation and profit maximization to the exclusion of where this leads in terms of long range consumer interest and human welfare, is at best unprofessional, at worst, irresponsible. The marketing fraternity has to respond collegially and sectorally to the challenge of orienting the discipline to gainfully build conserver values and replace prevailing consumption practices.

Marketing can play a rewarding role in a conserver society if managers and academia join hands to form an ad hoc group or to promote a **'Centre for Conserver Marketing'** for collegial planning and research and to undertake the necessary action. Initially, new rules in the form of a voluntary code of conduct could also be developed to make conservation the guiding objective. Emphasis will have to be placed on the benefits for the customers and employees, and sensible adjustment will have to be made to long term expectation of slow overall growth.

REFERENCES

1. Cater, Steve, "Marketing in Less Developed Countries – Time for

Dedicated Marketing Systems Not Adaptive Transfer?", *Public Enterprise*, 6, Feb, 1986, pp. 107-120.

2. Chakraborty, Satyesh C., "Dynamism in Environment Management : Its Relevance in Understanding the Importance of Conflict Resolution," *Decision*, 15, Jan-Mar, 1988, pp. 1-19.

3. Cracco, Etienne and Rostenne, Jacques, "The Socio-ecological Product", *MSU Business Topics*, 19, Summer, 1971, pp. 28-29.

4. Cravens, David W., "Marketing Management in an Era of Shortages," *Business Horizons*, 17, Feb 1974, pp. 79-85.

5. Dholakia, Nikhilesh, "Marketing in the Less Developed Countries : Its Nature and Prospects", in GS Kindra (ed), *Marketing in Developing Countries*, London and Sydney. Croom Helm, 1984, pp. 10-28.

6. Drucker, Peter F., "Converting Social Problems into Business Opportunities : The New Meaning of Corporate Social Responsibility", *California Management Review*, 26, Winter, 1984, pp. 53-63.

7. Fisk, George, *Marketing and the Ecological Crisis*, New York : Harper and Row, 1974.

8. Galbraith, Jay, *Organization Design*, Boston, Addison-Wesley, 1977.

9. Garett, Dennis E., "The Effectiveness of Marketing Policy Boycotts : Environmental Opposition to Marketing", *Journal of Marketing*, 51, April, 1987, pp. 46-57.

10. Ghosh, D.N., "Corporate Sector as the Creative Agent for Change", *address at the 30th Annual Convocation at the Xavier Labour Relations Institute, Jamshedpur*, March 5, 1988.

11. Hanna, N, et al, "Marketing Strategy Under Conditions of Economic Scarcity", *Journal of Marketing*, 39, Jan, 1975, pp. 63-67.

12. Henion, Karl E, II, *Ecological Marketing*, Columbus, Ohio : Grid, 1976.

13. Kinsey, J., "The Role of Marketing in Economic Development", *European Journal of Marketing*, 16, 6, 1982, pp. 151-152.

14. Kotler, Philip, "The Role of Marketing in Development", *Proceedings of the International Conference on Marketing and Development*, Istanbul, Turkey, September 1-4, 1986.

15. Kotler, Philip and Levy, Sidney, J., "Demarketing, Yes, Demarketing"; *Harvard Business Review*, 49, Nov-Dec, 1971, pp. 70-80.

16. Maurya, C., *unpublished project report for Tungbhadra Industries Ltd*, Kashi Vidyapeeth, Varanasi, 1985.

17. Parvatiyar, Atul, "Mood Marketing", *Business World*, May 9-22, 1988, p. 25.

18. Parvatiyar, Atul, "Dimensions of Future Marketing in India", *Management and Labour Studies*, 13, Jan, 1988, pp. 33-39.

19. Parvatiyar, Atul, "Conserver-Marketing", *Proceedings of II Inter-Institutional Meet of Marketing Managers and Instructors*, Varanasi, April 20-21, 1986.

20. Perry, Donald L., *Social Marketing Strategies : Conservation Issues and Analysis*, Pacific Palisades, California : Goodyear, 1976.

21. Rao, V.R., "Ecological Consequences and Marketing Implications : Bhopal Tragedy Aftermath", *unpublished report for the MMS Programme*, BHU, Varanasi, 1984.

22. Riley, H. Slater et al, "Food Marketing in the Economic Development of Puerto Rico", *Research Report No. 4, Latin American Studies Centre*, Michigan State University, 1983.

23. Rotenberg, Ronald H., "A New Role for Marketing in an Age of Scarcity", *Concordia University Working Paper* (mimeographed), 1975, pp. 13-14.

24. Rothe, James T. and Benson, Lissa, "Intelligent Consumption : An Attractive Alternative to the Marketing Concept", *MSU Business Topics*, 22, Winter, 1974, pp. 29-34.

25. Shapiro, Stanely J., "Marketing in a Conserver Society", *Business Horizons*, 21, April, 1978, pp. 3-13.

26. World Commission on Environment and Development – WCED (1987), *Our Common Future*, Delhi, Oxford and New York, Oxford University Press.

27. Zeithaml and Zeithaml, "Environmental Management : Revising the Marketing Perspective", *Journal of Marketing*, 48, Spring, 1984, pp. 46-53.

NOTES

1. The Conserver Movement can be defined as an "organised movement of concerned citizens and governments for conservation of scarce world resources and to protect and enhance people's living environment. Several Organizations like the Science Council of Canada; Committee for Environmental Protection, Bulgaria; NGO Network for Forest Conservation, Indonesia; Friends of the Earth and Ministeries of Environmental Protection and Conservation are fostering the conserver movement worldwide.

2. Some Studies that have been conducted on the ecological perspective in marketing are by Cravens (1974); Fish (1974); Rothe and Benson (1974); Hanna, et al (1975); Henion (1976); and Perry (1976).

3. The WCED Report (1987) presents a strong case for revival and change in the quality of economic growth. It favours a change in the orientation of technological development and in the direction of investments and institutional change.

4. The impact of poverty, shortages and degradation of the agricultural and water resource base all over the world may reduce the per capita production of food and therefore the incomes and earnings of people in the countries dependent on agriculture. This may marginalize people and force them to further destroy the resource base for survival. Therefore, demand patterns are likely to be distorted and shortages may lead to increase in food and agricultural prices leading to inflationary conditions.

5. Full cost pricing is more soundly based upon the realities of the stock capital that sustain it. For example, income from forestry operations and other products extracted, minus the costs of extraction. The costs of regenerating the forests are not taken into account, unless money is actually spent on such work. Full cost pricing requires the inclusion of all relevant social costs in the price of the product.

6. Some studies have been conducted to find out whether consumers are willing to change their life-styles and shift demand away from ecologically harmful products (Rao 1984; Maurya 1985).

Courtesy : Management and Labour Studies, Vol. 15. No. 2, April 1990.

Bibliography

Books

Aker, D.A. and Day, G.S., *Marketing Research*, John Willey and Sons Inc., New York, 1982.

Banner, W.H., *Successful Marketing*, Prentice-Hall, Inc., Englewood Cliffs, New Jersey, 1978.

Bennet, D. Peter, *Marketing*, McGraw-Hill Co., 1988.

Bhalla, G.S. and Alagh Y.K., *Performance of Indian Agriculture - A District-wise Study*, Sterling Publisher Pvt. Ltd., New Delhi, 1979.

Bolen, W.H., *Advertising*, John Willey and Sons, Inc., New York, 1982.

Davar, R.S., *Modern Marketing Management*, Crown Publishing House, Bombay, 1986.

Davis, E.J., *Experimental Marketing*, D.B. Taraparewala and Sons and Co. Pvt. Ltd., Bombay, 1982.

Davis, K.R., *Marketing Management*, John Willey, New York, 1982.

Dhindsa, K.S., *India's Export Performance: Some Policy Implications*, Intellectual Publishing House, New Delhi, 1981.

Drucker F. Peter, *The Practice of Management*, Allied

Publishers Ltd., New Delhi, 1988.

Fisk, George, *Marketing and the Ecological Crisis*, Harper and Row, New York, 1974.

Gandhi, J.C., *Marketing - A Managerial Introduction*, McGraw Hill Publishing Co., New Delhi, 1989.

Heller, R., *The Naked Market: Methods for the 1980s*, Sidgwick & Jackson, London, 1985.

Kayank Erderner, *Marketing in the Third World*, Praeger, New York, 1982.

Kindra, G.S. (ed), *Marketing in Developing Countries*, Croom Helton, London and Sydeny, 1984.

Kotler, Philip, *Marketing Management: Analysis, Planning and Control*, Prentice-Hall of India, New Delhi, 1988.

Kumar, Maneet, *Export Marketing of Non-traditional Items*, Ajanta Publications, New Delhi, 1986.

Luck J. David and Rubin S. Ronald, *Marketing Research*, Prentice Hall of India Pvt. Ltd., New Delhi, 1989.

Majaro, Simon, *International Marketing: A Strategic Approach to World Markets*, George Allen and Unwin Ltd., London, 1982.

Mathur, Navin, *Advertising and Consumer Reaction in India*, Printwell Publishers, Jaipur, 1986.

Meiden, Arthur, *Bank Marketing Management*, McMillan Studies in Marketing Management, 1984.

Neelamegham, S. (ed.), *Marketing Management and the Indian Economy*, Vikash Publishing House, Pvt. Ltd., New Delhi, 1979.

Perry R. Donald, *Social Marketing Strategies : Conservation Issues and Analysis*, Good Year, Pacific Palisades, California, 1976.

Rajbahak, R.P., et al (ed.), *Export Strategies, of 90s*, Anmol

Publications, New Delhi, 1990.

Rao C.H. Hanumantha, *Technological Change and Distribution of Grains in Indian Agriculture*, Institute of Economic Growth, New Delhi.

Schultz, T.W., *Transforming Traditional Agriculture*, Yale University Press, New Haven, 1964.

Singh, M.K. and Mahadevan Anant, (ed.), *Export Management*, Discovery Publishing House, New Delhi, 1990.

Saxena, K.K., *Bank Marketing: Concepts and Applications*, Skylark Publications, New Delhi, 1986.

Twedt W. Dick (ed.), *A Survey of Marketing Research*, American Marketing Association, Chicago, 1973.

Articles

Agrawal, M.L., "Marketing in the Ancillary Industries," *Indian Management*, December, 1987.

---------. "Marketing of Health Food in Europe : Is the Experience Replicable in India"?, *Management and Labour Studies*, July, 1989.

Ahamad, Abrar, "Emerging Dimensions of Marketing Management in India", *Proceedings of Second Inter-Institutional Meet of Marketing Managers and Instructors, Varanasi*, April, 1986.

Ayer S. Bhaskar, "The Coming of Qualitative Research", *Business World*, November 8-21, 1989.

Bajaj, Ramakrishna, "New Challenge Before Industry", *Times of India*, New Delhi, May 23, 1990.

Bhattacharya, B.N. and Ghose, B.K., "Marketing of Banking Services in the 90s: Problems and Perspectives," *Economic and Political Weekly*, February 25, 1989.

Buskirk, R.H. and Rothe, J.T., "Consumerism — An Interpretation," *Journal of Marketing*, Vol. 24, October, 1979.

Chakraborty C. Satyesh, "Dynamism in Environment Management: Its Relevance in Understanding the Importance of Conflict Resolution," *Decision*, 15, Jan.-Mar., 1988.

Ghose, B.K., "Bank Nationalisation - Premises and Performances," *The Journal of Indian Institute of Bankers*, July-September, 1987.

Kaushik, Meena, "The Use of Qualitative Research in Developing and Testing Advertisement," *Deccan Herald*, Bangalore, 1987.

Khanna, K.M., "The Changing Advertising Scene," *Proceedings of the Advertising Seminar Organised by Deccan Herald*, Bangalore, 1987.

Kotler, Philip, "From Sales Obsession to Marketing Effectiveness," *Harvard Business Review*, Nov-Dec., 1987.

Langer, Judith, "At Last Marketers Acknowledge Women's Role," *Marketing News*, AMA, Chicago, November 8, 1985.

Parvatiyar, Atul, "Mood Marketing", *Bussiness World*, May 9-22, 1988.

Rao, V.K.B., "Marketing of Bank Services," *Indian Journal of Marketing*, September, 1986.

Shapiro J. Stanely, "Marketing in a Conserver Society", *Business Horizons*, April 21, 1978.

Singh, Ajit, "Training for Bank Marketing," *Financial Express*, Bombay, December 31, 1986.

Traynor, Keenneth, "Research Deserves Status as Marketing's Fifth `P'," *Marketing News*, AMA, Chicago,

November 8, 1985.

Vieria, Walter, "Emerging Market for the Very Riches," *Business World*, November 9-22, 1987.

Zeithaml and Zeithaml, "Environmental Management Revising the Marketing Perspective," *Journal of Marketing*, 48, Spring, 1984.

Periodicals and other Publications

Advertising Age

Atlanta Economic Review

Business India

Business Week

Census 1981

Economic Survey 1989-90, Government of India.

Foreign Trade Bulletin.

Harvard Business Review

India 1988.

Report of the Registrar of News Papers of India - 1988.

Yojana

Vikalpa.

INDEX

About The Editors . . .

S.C. Sahoo (b. 1941) is Professor of Management, teaching at the Berhampur University, Berhampur, Orissa, India. He was, earlier, an Associate Professor in Marketing at the Xavier Institute of Management, Bhubaneswar. He received his Master's Degree in 1965 and Ph.D. in 1975 from Utkal University, India.

Beside publishing a number of research articles, Dr. Sahoo has, to his credit, two very popular books for the undergraduate students : (i) Groundwork of Salesmanship (Oriya) and (ii) Salesmanship, Sales Management and Advertising. While three of Prof. Sahoo's scholars have been awarded Ph.D. degrees seven are presently working under his guidance for Doctoral studies.

Prof. Sahoo's areas of interest include Export Marketing, Sales and Distribution Management and Rural Marketing.

P.K. Sinha (b. 1960) is an Associate Professor at the Xavier Institute of Management, Bhubaneswar, in the area of Marketing. Dr. Sinha has a Doctorate in Marketing and offers courses on Service Marketing, Marketing Research, Rural Marketing & Sales and Distribution Management. His research articles have been published in various reputed journals in India.

Contd....